THE BEST YEARS OF OUR LIVES

A History of Education in Bishop Monkton

A Joint Project by Bishop Monkton Church of England Primary School and Bishop Monkton Local History Group

Edited by

Colin Philpott

Fisher King Publishing

THE BEST YEARS OF OUR LIVES

Published by Fisher King Publishing
fisherkingpublishing.co.uk

PREFACE

This book is part of a project involving Bishop Monkton Primary School and Bishop Monkton Local History Group. It was undertaken in 2024 and 2025 to research and record the history of education in the village.

It covers both the village school and the former Mechanics' Institution, once a centre for adult education. The project involves the production of this book, a film, an exhibition and content for websites, as well as the provision of learning materials for lessons in the School.

This book is dedicated to the memory of all those who have contributed over a period of almost 200 years to the education of Bishop Monkton's children and its adults.

Contents

FOREWORD

I feel truly privileged to be a part of the rich history of Bishop Monkton School. As the current headteacher, I not only see myself as an integral part of the School's journey but also as a caretaker for the generations that will follow. Our School has a proud legacy, and it is an honour to contribute to its ongoing story, ensuring that the values and traditions that have shaped this place continue to inspire future learners. The School was first established by the church as a place to educate the poor children of the village. Although our community may have changed, still at the heart of our school is a desire to equip the next generation with skills for success.

Bishop Monkton School has always been a warm, welcoming place – a large family that creates a sense of belonging for us all. One inspector, on arrival into School, described it as *'being embraced by a warm hug'.* I hope you gain a sense of this as you pass through the history of our School.

From when I was a child there has been a massive shift in pupil and parent voice. Looking back at the history of the School there were definitely times when children were not free to express themselves, nor parents able to approach the school gate without prior arrangement. The open-door policy of today's education is far removed from Victorian attitudes. I wonder what the first woman headteacher, Miss Shippam (1916-1939) would make of the weekly hot chocolate and biscuits which I share with those children who have been chosen as Star of the Week!

Children who have passed through Bishop Monkton School may remember their musical opportunities, their sporting glory, the sense of achievement when they finally mastered a skill, the progress they made in reading, writing or maths or the knowledge they learned about Mayan civilisation. More than this, I hope children remember the feeling of being at Bishop Monkton School – a place where they were encouraged to be their best version, where they felt cared for and safe to be themselves.

I hope you enjoy sharing in the journey of Bishop Monkton CE Primary School.

Sally A. Cowling
Headteacher 2009 to date

2023 OFSTED Report Celebrations

Head, Sally Cowling celebrates with some of her pupils, a GOOD OFSTED Report

INTRODUCTION
A story with many threads

At first sight, the story of education in the North Yorkshire village of Bishop Monkton might seem a rather straightforward matter. A village school opened here in 1849 and it is still here in 2025, having acquired a new site in 1971. It is just one of more than 16,000 primary schools in England. However, behind these bare facts, there is so much more to the story. The development of the School is inextricably interwoven with changes, social, economic and cultural, in Bishop Monkton over the past two centuries. It is also, in microcosm, part of a national story – the story of how education itself, and the ideas underpinning it, have developed across the country in the last 200 years.

The Original School - opened in 1849

Photo from the 1950's, the frontage had been virtually unchanged

In addition, this is a story which is not just about our village school. It also touches on a number of other, private schools which we believe existed here, for which there is reasonable evidence and for which we can identify their probable locations. Also, it is not just about the education of children. The Mechanics' Institution, opened in 1859, founded on the Victorian ideal of self-improvement for the working classes, provided adult education here for more than a century. The 'Mickey', as it was affectionately known, was unusual for such a small community. Most Mechanics' Institutions were concentrated in towns and cities, mainly across the North of England.

Most importantly, this is a story which is much more than an account of buildings, of political systems and structures, of educational theories and challenges. It is a human story of pupils, teachers and staff, parents, governors and others who helped shape, and were themselves shaped, by education in one North Yorkshire community.

Many themes emerge from this: –

- How the School has gone from teaching the children of the agricultural poor of the village to the education of the overwhelmingly middle-class children of today, roughly half of whom come from outside the village.
- How schooling here started in an era when the very idea of educating the children of the poor was controversial with fears that this would encourage the 'lower orders' to 'rise above their station.'
- How the role and influence of the churches, particularly the

Church of England, was very dominant in the creation and development of the School in the nineteenth century and which remained significant in the twentieth and even into the twenty-first century.

- How just getting children to turn up to school was the main struggle for first few decades of the School's existence with education seen as desirable but not necessarily the top priority in an economy still then making use of child labour.
- How the standard of teachers, the facilities for teaching and the curriculum have developed beyond all recognition since the early days of the School.
- How the personalities and priorities of headteachers has been crucial in the running of the School.
- How accountability and inspection regimes, as well as the involvement of parents in the running of the school, have developed.

1988 Summer - The School - Pupils, Teachers & other Staff

Fortunately, there is a decent amount of written and visual material which helps to tell this story but also many people still around whose memories help bring this history to life. Our sources have included the local archives for North and for West Yorkshire, the log books and other records kept by the School itself, and two earlier publications about village history. In addition, we have benefitted from the expert knowledge of several people with an academic interest in education and, particularly, the recollections and memories of pupils, staff, parents, governors and others.

Our account of education is divided into four main parts. In Chapter One, we describe the period up to 1900 including the setting up of the village school but also including what we know about other schools in Bishop Monkton. In Chapter Two, we move on to the period from 1900 to 1971, the year when the School moved to its present site. In Chapter Three, we move from 1971 to the present day. Each of the first three chapters starts with a short list of key dates during the period it covers, as well as a list of headteachers for the period. Chapter Four focuses on the story of the Mechanics' Institution.

It has not been possible to identify everyone in some class photographs included in the book. These are indicated with a ? in the captions.

We hope this book will give people a greater understanding and appreciation of how Bishop Monkton has taught its young, and its grown-ups, over the past two centuries. Above all, we hope you find it entertaining as well as illuminating.

Colin Philpott

CHAPTER ONE – BEFORE 1900
The Opening of Bishop Monkton School and what went before

Headteachers

1849-1869	J P Wheeler
1869-1887	John Newman
1887-1890	Reynold Andrew Cuthbert
1890-1916	Smith Jowett

Key Dates

1811 Church of England established the National Society for Promoting the Education of the Poor in the Principles of the Established Church (the National Society).

1814 Non-conformists set up British and Foreign School Society.

1833 Parliament voted sums of money each year for the construction of schools for poor children, the first time the state had become involved with education in England and Wales.

1839 Government grants for the construction and maintenance of schools were switched to voluntary bodies and became conditional on a satisfactory inspection.

1849 School set up in Bishop Monkton by Church of England, originally known as 'St. John's National School'.

1870 Education Act, the 'Forster Act' introduced compulsory universal education for children aged five to twelve but left enforcement of attendance to school boards.

Private Schools

It is unlikely that we will ever know exactly when the first schooling of any type took place in Bishop Monkton. However, there is some partial evidence of schools existing some time before the establishment in 1849 of what we now know as Bishop Monkton Primary School.

The earliest known mention of education of any sort in the village dates from May 1700. A document in the West Yorkshire Archives includes a recommendation for William Hardcastle, described as a 'schoolmaster of Bishop Monkton,' for his application to be Curate of Arkendale Parish Church. The great and good of Bishop Monkton and Ripon at the time 'believe him to be a person of sober life and comfortable to the doctrine and discipline of the Church of England.'

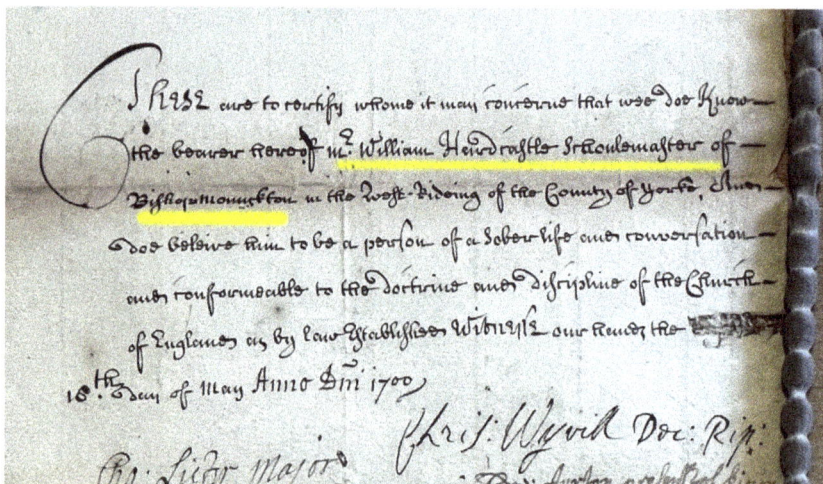

William Hardcastle, Schoolmaster of Bishop Monkton

The recommendation was signed by the Mayor of Ripon, Charles Lister among fourteen others, and it is therefore perhaps not surprising that he was successful in his application. He went on to be Curate at Arkendale for many years. Nothing more is known about him nor anything about the school where he taught but the description 'schoolmaster of Bishop Monkton' gives us some reason to believe that there might have been a school here in the early 1700s.

Another fascinating snippet which also raises more questions than it answers was uncovered in the North Yorkshire County Record Office. Lodged there is a copy of a school project completed in November 1848 by Abraham Swales, a twelve year old boy from Bishop Monkton.

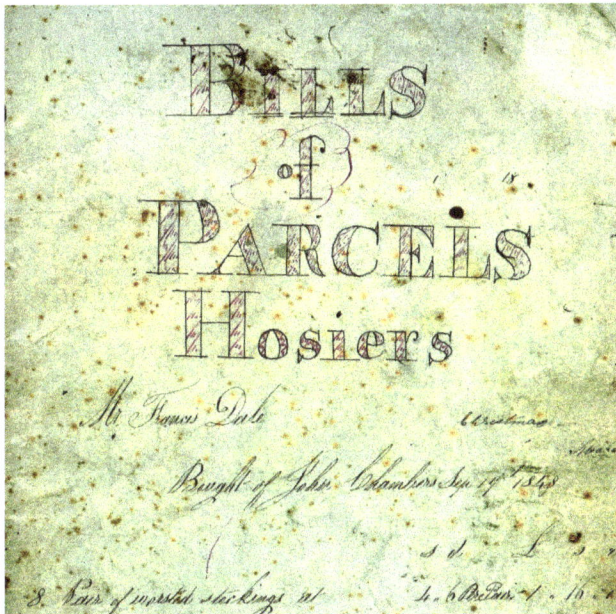

Abraham Swales - extract - Francis Dale, Hosiers, sales

The project was, in effect, a study of the economy of the village listing various tradespeople who worked here with details of what they did. The study demonstrated a strong command of arithmetic with many calculations of weights and measures and he was obviously a very clever boy for his age. Little else is known about him except that, in 1871 by the age of thirty-five, he was an Officer of the Inland Revenue with a wife and two children living in Shipley. What is unclear is where he was taught as a child or who asked him to undertake the project. Could he have been studying at a school in the village? Intriguingly, the project was completed just a year before Bishop Monkton School opened.

Abraham Swales - extracts - 4 more local traders showing some of their sales

There are other tantalising glimpses of schools existing in the village before 1849 and indeed of schools which may have existed after that date alongside the main village school. Mary Gertrude Butterfield's book, 'Bishop Monkton and Environs', published in 1958, mentions four locations in the village which were said to have been so-called 'Dame Schools'.

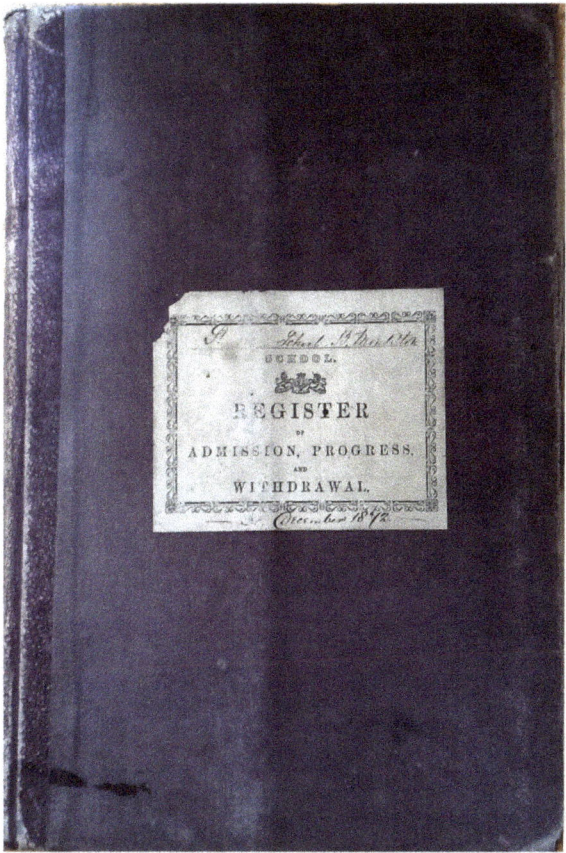

Register of Admissions, Progress, and Withdrawal - December 1874

According to Butterfield, the dame schools were run by the Misses Wilkinson at Rose Cottage, by the Misses Sophia and Jane Ward at Hawthorn House, by Mrs. Mary Heath at Hungate House and by Miss Frances Sadler at the Limes, and later by Miss Swires. Another record, however, describes Mary Heath's establishment as a 'Ladies' Seminary'. There is also one entry in the local Standard School Register of Admissions and Withdrawals of an 'Albert Chambers, son of a Shop Keeper, in March 1874, age five years, six months', whose means of 'Previous Instruction' was entered as 'Dame School.'

Albert Chambers, listed in this Register of Admissions in 1874, whose 'previous instructions' were listed as 'Dame School'

Dame schools were a significant phenomenon in educational provision in England, as well as in Australia and the United States, from the seventeenth to the mid-nineteenth centuries. They were private, elementary schools with, in most cases, women as teachers. They were largely found in towns and local parishes and were run initially for two to five year olds, taught by a 'school dame', a local woman. She would teach ABCs, arithmetic and sometimes writing. In addition, girls were taught knitting and sewing.

It is thought that dame schools may have evolved from a demand for cheap childcare and early rudimentary education. Teaching would often take place in the teacher's home, being independently run by women in the local area rather than through a network. Many of these women were either older, unmarried women, or young, unmarried women or impoverished middle class widows, all of whom needed an additional income. Hardly any of these schools were staffed by men.

The schools only charged a meagre fee of a few shillings a year suggesting that pupils received very little in return. Pupils were mainly the children of labouring parents and tradesmen and these schools provided the only education they ever received. Reading and writing was mainly done from a 'hornbook', a teaching aid consisting of a leaf of paper showing the alphabet, and often the ten digits and the Lord's Prayer, mounted on a wooden tablet and protected by a thin plate of horn. Both boys and girls were usually taught to read, although generally only boys were taught to write. However, in the eighteenth century, there was a rising movement which discouraged working class children to write. As a result some dame schools subsequently did not teach any writing to either boys or girls.

Reading the Bible was an essential, religious obligation, so learning to read was important. Some dame schools would teach the catechism or would invite the local clergyman to do so. Teaching rudimentary arithmetic was provided to enable the pupils to learn the operating of household accounts.

By the eighteenth-century, dame schools appear to have been widely spread across England but, due to the informal nature of these schools, it was difficult to estimate the exact number as documentation was scarce. In Yorkshire, out of 836 villages surveyed, one in forty had dame schools, including it would appear, Bishop Monkton.

Hawthorn House - location of Dame School

The industrialisation of the nineteenth-century changed the role of dame schools. More and more parents worked in factories, and dame schools provided a cheap form of childcare. In fact some of the schools offered just childcare whilst others offered a basic education as well. However, as the Victorian era wore on, competitors to dame schools were developing. The Sunday School movement arose at this time, where children would go to school on Sundays to learn religious lessons and basic literacy. Private philanthropists established free schools specifically to educate lower class children. Most significantly, social reformers and politicians were focussing on reforming the educational system into a national, standardised and compulsory system and away from small, localised educational institutions.

Village Farmhouse - location of Dame School

For a while, many parents were unhappy with this idea, and they continued to send their children to dame schools. Dame schools were more informal, and operated in the kind of homes the children were familiar with and gave parents more control over their schooling.

As late as 1850 around thirty percent of children attended dame schools but they largely closed down following the Newcastle Commission in 1861 which painted a woeful portrait of their inadequacy. When the Elementary Education Act of 1870 introduced compulsory education, dame schools were closed as there were now new educational facilities in place for children.

The Limes - location of Dame School

There are two other pieces of evidence about private schools in Bishop Monkton. Clare Royds, who has lived in the village most of her life, is certain that Village Farm on Hungate used to be a girls' school when it was a single storey building. Examination of the building now reveals that the upper storey is made of different materials and appears to be a later addition.

In addition, it appears that at least one private school was operating in the village in the 1870s – more than twenty years after the regular public village school had opened. An entry in the Bishop Monkton School Logbook on 10th November, 1871, notes that, 'Some of the children of dissenting parents have left to go to a new private school in the village.' On 28th June, 1878, another entry in the log recorded that, 'The private school in the village having closed, several of the children were admitted on Monday.' The logs also record attempts, apparently unsuccessful, in 1879 and 1880 to set up a school attached to the Wesleyan Chapel.

Why Bishop Monkton School was set up

However, the most important event in developing education in Bishop Monkton was the establishment of a school in 1849. A series of economic, political, social, and religious factors, which impacted on Victorian England as a whole, led to the setting up of the School in the village and these factors are important in the understanding of how the School came into existence.

As the nineteenth-century advanced, England began to see that its provision of education was neither adequate to meet the country's fast growing industrial needs nor to maintain its future prospects as a great European power. Literacy was growing, but not fast enough. For liberal thinkers, particularly among Nonconformists, one solution came to be seen to lie in schools which would have a particular focus on the labouring classes for whom education had neither been affordable nor had been seen as necessary to earn a living.

On the other hand, the middle and upper classes had the means to educate their own children privately and feared that educating the 'unlettered' might disturb the social balance and even risk the revolutions that had racked the European Continent for the previous half century. These fears were particularly felt by Tory landowners and in villages whose ancestral wealth derived from the rural population.

There were strident voices arguing against the education of the poor. When the Parochial Schools Bill of 1807 was debated in Parliament, MP Davies Giddy (later Gilbert), President of the Royal Society, warned the House of Commons: "However specious in theory the project might be of giving education to the labouring classes of the poor, it would, in effect, be found to be prejudicial to their morals and happiness; it would teach them to despise their lot in life, instead of making them good servants in agriculture and other laborious employments to which their rank in society had destined them."

Change, however, could not be denied and its success was going to depend on money from the government and a backbone of support from the churches. The tipping point for education in England was the passage of the Great Reform Act of 1832 which broadened the electoral franchise. The following seven decades until the Education Act of 1902 saw a schooling system develop into a recognisable modern form. Bishop Monkton played its part in this change, despite being a tiny rural community engaged in growing wheat and barley and manufacturing flax and paper products and numbering only 435 citizens at the census of 1851.

The Church of England was a leading player in this educational development. For three centuries since the Reformation, its bishops had seen their institution as the guardian of the nation's spiritual health and therefore of necessity also of its education. They were now feeling pressure from the growing Nonconformist communities, who sought to meet the moral and intellectual needs of congregations engaged in the rapidly advancing industrial revolution. The Nonconformists were ambitious for education to develop but did not want it to do so under the control of the established Anglican church. Each protagonist in this debate established its competing campaign groups. In 1811 the Anglican bishops set up the National Society for Promoting the Education of the Poor and in 1814 a group of Nonconformists founded the British and Foreign School Society for the Education of the Labouring and Manufacturing Classes, both aiming to build new schools.

Around 1900

In 1833, two decades after these societies were created, the government in Westminster allocated its first funds aimed at supporting the school building plans of the two societies. It did not, however, intend to intervene between these rivals nor take a lead for fear of promoting one religious group over another and made a decision that the grants would be made to all recognised religious denominations. This enduring policy was subsequently summarised in the pivotal Elementary Education Act of 1870, which stated that, 'No religious catechism or religious formulary which is distinctive of any particular denomination shall be taught in the school.'

The 1833 government grant was a modest and cautious amount of £20,000 in total for the whole country (about £3m at 2025 values) but future grants were made annually and would grow year by year to support efforts of the religious bodies to build and maintain schools and to train teachers. The Church of England, with its nationwide web of parishes, was by far the larger of the two church societies and thus benefitted most from the early grants. It accordingly set the National Society the aim of providing a school in every parish and by 1850 the Society had founded 12,000 schools.

How Bishop Monkton School was set up

Despite its small population, Bishop Monkton was felt worthy to have one of these new schools, perhaps partly because the living of St. John's had always been in the gift of the Dean and Chapter of Ripon Cathedral, which lay only three miles from the village. Its vicar in the mid-1840s, the Rev. Robert Poole, duly set about establishing the school and applied for a government grant.

Government funding then carried conditions, as it does now, and those for the grant had been set out by the Treasury in 1839. The vicar accordingly had to follow the due process. No grant could be considered unless voluntary contributions equal to half the total estimated expenditure had been received and would be spent on building a new school. In the case of Bishop Monkton, the principal benefactor was Elizabeth Sophia Lawrence, a descendant of William Aislabie, who owned and managed her ancestor's Studley Royal estates from 1808 until her death in 1845.

She had accordingly inherited vast wealth and so was able to be a steadfast benefactor of Ripon and its surrounding region. Her charitable works included the building of the town's cottage hospital, a school in Sharow, and several churches, and it was she who gifted the land on which the school at Bishop Monkton was built. The building was on St. John's Road, across from the beck, two doors down from the site of the current school, in what is now a private house, appropriately called the Old School House. When it opened it was originally known as St. John's National School.

Also, the Treasury required the deed setting up the proposed school to declare the premises to be granted in trust for the education of the poor and for no other purpose whatsoever. The deed also provided for the legal ownership of the premises, proposed that the school's management should be according to precedents settled for the Church of England, and required annual visits by government inspectors. The application also had to be accompanied by a report from the National Society confirming that the proposal presented a worthy case and that there was a reasonable expectation that the school would be permanently supported. The application succeeded and in 1849 the village school was opened. The churchwardens of St. John's were to be its trustees and the successive incumbents of the living, the Anglican minister in the village, were to be appointed chairmen of the school's managers.

What was the School like?

Teaching standards and expectations were low. By the time they left school the children were expected to know their catechism, read the Bible and maybe a newspaper. Writing standards were poor, maybe enough to write a letter home if working away but that was all. Girls spent their afternoons sewing and knitting and boys doing extra sums or drawing.

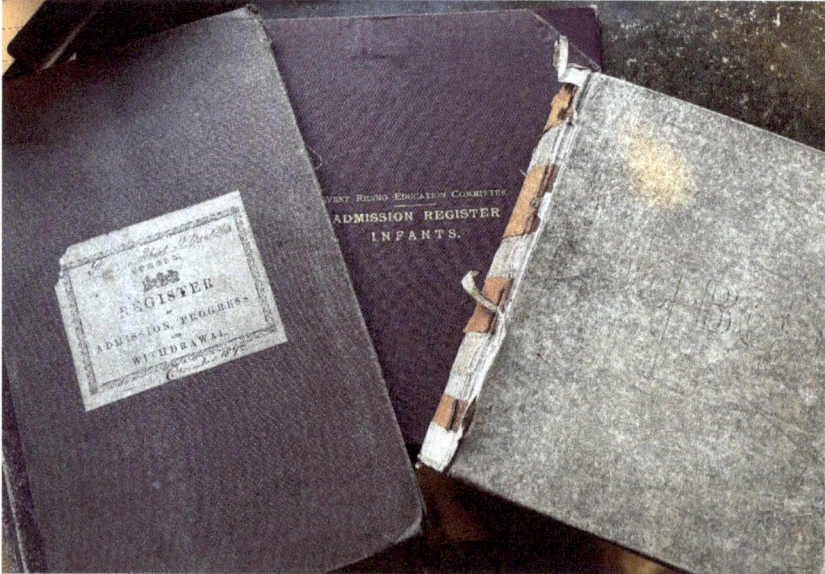

Register & Log Books

However, it was no easy task trying to teach the pupils. Children were persistently absent, harvesting, blackberrying, looking for work or just helping at home. Without enough attendances a child did not count for grant purposes, so much of the teachers' time was spent in getting pupils back to school. It is difficult for us in the twenty-first century, where attendance is compulsory and accepted as necessary by the vast majority of people, to imagine a world where most people, particularly the agricultural poor in a place like Bishop Monkton, saw school as desirable but not essential. The log books from the early decades of Bishop Monkton School demonstrate just how much time had to be put into achieving reasonable levels of school attendance.

Officially sanctioned reasons for allowing absence or even for closing the School completely make for interesting reading. They included:- a day's holiday on 22nd April 1870 for the Mechanics' Institute Soiree; a three week holiday once harvest had started; the School closed for a week when the Master's mother died. But the reasons given for unauthorised absence are even more interesting, including:- going to see the foxhunt in the village, rabbit shooting, house cleaning by girls in April, working in the gardens by boys in April, attending various events in the village including cricket matches, fairs, and flower shows.

The School had only four headmasters from its founding right through until the First World War and, just as importantly three vicars, of whom the Reverend F. J. Poole and his son were central to the development and running of the school and discipline within it. He was not only the Vicar from 1865 to 1898 but also Chairman of the managers of the School. He visited at least every week to give lessons and ensure that religious education played a significant part in the life of the School.

It was no easy life being the headmaster of this School. John Newman was here at Bishop Monkton for eighteen years with his wife Clara as his assistant. It was a time of much change in education, but he had his work cut out as these extracts from the School logbook show: -

1875

August 20th – The Davys returned to school after an absence of three months caused by their being offended in Sunday School. Harvest being now general it was thought advisable to break up for holidays. School holidays were variable depending on weather for the harvest. Rev. Poole visited the school.

Sept. 24th - Reopened the school with a fair attendance chiefly of girls and infants. Tested them individually. Sent after absentees.

Oct. 1st - Admitted two Wigglesworths, very backward boys. Kemp played truant again on Wednesday and Thursday, punished him on Friday. Rev. Poole visited the school on Monday.

Oct. 8th - Holiday on Monday afternoon, Monkton Fair. Re-admitted A. and M. Dobby. Home lessons unsatisfactory. Lent slates to those children who had none of their own. Rev. F. P. visited the school on Wednesday and Friday.

Oct. 15th - Attendance improved, probably in consequence of the Harvest Festival.

What were lessons like?

The School could be quite a grim building. The rooms were warmed by a single stove or open fire. The walls of a Victorian schoolroom were quite bare, except perhaps for an embroidered text. Curtains were used to divide the schoolhouse into classrooms. The shouts of several classes competed as they were taught side by side. There was little fresh air because the windows were built high in the walls, to stop pupils looking outside and being distracted from their work.

Children learned to write on slates and they scratched letters on them with sharpened pieces of slate. Paper was expensive, but slates could be used again and again. Children were supposed to bring sponges to clean them. Most just spat on the slates and rubbed them clean with their sleeves. Older children learned to use pen and ink by writing in 'copybooks.' Each morning the ink monitor filled up little clay ink wells and handed them round from a tray. Pens were fitted with separate nibs and children were punished for spilling ink that 'blotted their copybooks.'

Slates showing pictures and names of different objects hung from the walls of the infants' class. The children chanted the name of each object in turn. When they could use these words in sentences they would move on to a 'reader.' Quicker readers fidgeted as they waited for their turn to read. A reader had to last for a whole year. If the class read it too quickly, they had to go back to the beginning and read it all over again!

The pupils used an abacus to help them with their maths. Calculations were made using imperial weights and measures instead of our simpler metric system. Children had to pass inspections in maths, reading and writing before they could move up to the next class or 'standard.' Teachers were also tested by the dreaded inspector, to make sure that they deserved government funds.

Overall, during the first few decades of its existence, the list of subjects covered in lessons at the School includes many we recognise and expect today but others which would look out of place in a modern curriculum. Subjects taught included Arithmetic, Religious Education, Needlework, Singing, Drawing, Catechism, Drill, the Geography of Palestine, Map of England, Grammar, Writing and Spelling of the Lord's Prayer, Reading Book of Judges in the Bible, Reading the Gospel of St. Luke in the Bible, Dictation, Alphabet Class, Home Lessons, the Geography of Canada, Clay Modelling, Temperance, Mat Weaving.

In Bishop Monkton School, as in other elementary schools, boys and girls typically entered the infants' class at the age of four and they would progress through the mixed class of older children from seven years old onwards. At the age of eleven, they could leave school to go to work or help in their home but they could stay until aged fourteen.

Classes were usually conducted by the Headteacher for the mixed class and the assistant for the infants. 'National' elementary schools like Bishop Monkton employed 'Bell's' monitorial system' for the mixed class. Under this system the School had a single large schoolroom, so that the master could keep the whole school under scrutiny. Desks facing the walls were used for writing drills, while the central area was used by groups of ten to twenty children standing for instruction by their monitor, usually with the aid of cards hanging on the wall.

The master taught the monitors, who were usually aged about ten or eleven, and the monitors then passed on this teaching to their groups, recommended pupils for promotion and kept order. Despite its obvious shortcomings, this system continued in use until the quality of education improved with a new approach to the training of teachers.

The infants were required to be 'instructed suitably to their age, and in a manner not to interfere with the instruction of the older children.'

For the children in the mixed class, the aim was to achieve adequate literacy by following a graded syllabus between the ages of seven and eleven. The grants to the School were conditional on attendance of each scholar as recorded in the School register and his or her progress as measured by examination. A full annual grant was given for each child who completed 200 morning or afternoon attendances of at least two hours during the school year, subject to reductions for failures at examinations on report from the School's government inspector.

The code set defined standards for each subject and for each year. For example, the reading standards were built around the reading books used in the School and were stated as:

1.   Narrative in monosyllables.
2.   One of the narratives next in order after monosyllables.
3.   A short paragraph from an elementary reading book.
4.   A short paragraph from a more advanced reading book.

5. A few lines of poetry from a book used in the first class.

6. A short ordinary paragraph in a newspaper, or other modern narrative.

These specific standards were not popular among teachers, who argued that using them as the basis for the annual grant led to scholars learning their books wholesale in order to pass their examinations, and hence to teachers being constrained to a process of 'payment by results'.

1898

The head, **Mr Jowett**, with his school pupils

Punishment and Sickness

Punishment for poor performance, as well as for bad behaviour, seems harsh viewed from the twenty-first century. Teachers handed out regular canings. Look inside the logbooks kept by the School and you will see many reasons for this:- rude conduct, leaving the playground without permission, sulkiness, answering back, fighting, throwing stones at a teacher, throwing caps in the beck, missing Sunday prayers, throwing ink pellets, causing disruption through apple eating and being late. Boys were caned across their bottoms, and girls across their hands or bare legs.

Punishment did not end with caning. In some schools, including almost certainly in Bishop Monkton, pupils who weren't learning quickly enough had to stand on a stool at the back of the class, wearing an arm band with DUNCE written on it. The teacher then took a tall, cone-shaped hat decorated with a large 'D' and placed it on the child's head. Today we know that some children learn more slowly than others. Victorian teachers believed that all children could learn at the same speed and, if some fell behind, then they should be punished for not trying hard enough.

Sickness was very common and there were concerns that compulsory schooling would make sickness worse. However, it wasn't until 1906 that school medical inspections were started along with the famous 'nit nurse.' Measles, whooping cough, diphtheria, 'scald head' (better known as ringworm), influenza and fevers often decimated attendance figures of the pupils but they were not alone. One mistress was reported as suffering from congestion of the brain and her life being in despair and a master suffering from deafness meant that he couldn't discipline his class because he couldn't hear the noise!

Headteachers' Struggles

At the end of his time here as Head, John Newman was obviously exhausted. His reports virtually ran out and his final inspection report said, 'This School is in a very unsatisfactory condition and the children have gained little by attending it.' The reports of inspectors who visited the School seemed to bear witness to the School's failings.

On June 26, 1885 an inspector wrote:- 'Handwriting and spelling are a little weak. Arithmetic, though improved, needs attention, as does also mental arithmetic. Sewing deserves praise. The results in English and Geography are not worth the time spent on them. In singing by rote, though the older children have made creditable progress, the younger are too backward to justify the higher grant. If the abandonment of the class subjects enabled the Master to cultivate a brighter tone in the School it might yet do well, for though the children are well behaved, yet there is a total lack of life in the working of the School.'

In 1887 Mr. R.A. Cuthbert took over and his first entry states, 'Thirty-seven children attended today. They are very disorderly and ill mannered... the infants are totally ignorant.'

Mr. Cuthbert was only Headmaster for three years and, whilst numbers on the register improved to eighty, average attendance was only fifty-one and the same problems of missing school to go to work continued. In September 1890, only nineteen boys out of thirty-four attended and later in the month the School was shut because 'so few scholars assembled this morning that school was closed for the remainder of the week.'

Mr. Cuthbert ceased his duties on 19th September 1890.

The School reopened in mid-October 1890 with a new Master, Mr. Smith Jowett, again with his wife as his assistant. Both were certified teachers. Smith Jowett was also not impressed by the standard of teaching. His first logbook notes say, 'The children are backward in their work; infants are very ignorant. No sewing has been taught for five months.' However, he was to stay for twenty-six years.

Smith Jowett came from Sheriff Hutton, and he brought his daughter and son with him. He was said to be a 'very true draughtsman' and his wife, who was mistress at the school, had 'remarkable artistry in stitchery and design'. It feels like this was the start of a modern schooling system for Bishop Monkton with teachers who were very accomplished. So much so that one of the village's most distinguished inhabitants was their son. Percy Jowett CBE was a famous artist, Principal of the Royal College of Art and Freeman of the City of London. Quite a step from Bishop Monkton! The School continued to grow and progress under their leadership. The log books show growing numbers and competence.

School attendance did improve by the turn of the century. The Kelly's Directory, which included a brief outline of each place in Britain, noted the average attendance numbers against the total school roll as follows – forty-nine out of ninety in 1889; sixty out of 109 in 1893; and eighty-five out of 109 in 1908.

In its first half century of existence Bishop Monkton School clearly had many challenges and struggled to provide a decent education in difficult circumstances. However, by the dawn of the new century, things appeared to be on the up.

CHAPTER TWO – 1900 TO 1971
Developing the School and
moving to a new site

Headteachers

1890-1916	Smith Jowett
1916-1939	Helena May Shippam
1939-1950	Miss E. Goss
1950-1956	Ada Mary Walters
1956 -1991	Doreen Willis

Key Dates

1902 – County Councils, including the West Riding County Council (Bishop Monkton was part of the West Riding until 1974), became local education authorities controlling schools.

1918 – Leaving age raised again to fourteen.

1939 – Bishop Monkton School welcomes wartime evacuees from Leeds and elsewhere.

1944 – Landmark Education Act brought in many changes to education including free school milk and requiring local authorities to provide school meals. Also brought Church of England Schools more fully into the state system.

1971 – Bishop Monkton School opened its new building but retained its original building (now the Old School House) and operated across both sites for the rest of the century.

The first recorded memories of the School

Throughout the first half of the twentieth-century Bishop Monkton School gradually developed its reputation and adapted as educational philosophies and Government requirements changed. By the end of this period, not long after the Second World War, the need for better and larger premises was already being discussed, although it would take until 1971 to bring this ambition to fruition.

1906

? Slater, Bob Hymas, ? Richardson, Roland Simpson, Tom Press, Harry Heath
Lilly Hutchinson, Miriam Press, Olive Harrison, Ada Heath, Beaty Vasey, Agnes Jones, Doris Slater, Bella Bellaby, Vida Simpson, Tom Bellaby
Mitchell, Mart Press, Minnie Bellaby, Lillian Vasey, Maud Vasey, Eva Daniel, Nellie Jones, Olive Simpson
Stanley Vasey, Lillian Daniel, Katy Jones, Gertie Slater, Ruth Daniel

The earliest recorded memories of life at the School known to be available date back to the very dawn of the 1900s. Ada Wilkinson's memories of attending the School from 1903 were written down by her family some years ago. The notes, which are still preserved today, help give a picture of what was clearly an experience of school quite different from what we would expect now, more than a century later.

1908

18 boys and 18 girls in this photograph which was seemingly taken at the same time as the picture on the next page (page 36) with the window reflections the same - a mystery?

Ada was born in November 1898 and lived at Glenroyd Cottages in the village. She started at Bishop Monkton School at the age of four and stated in her old age that she had not liked it. Her mother used to take her halfway and then she was passed into the care of the headteacher, Mr. Jowett. She said everyone liked his wife, Mrs. Jowett, because she was sweet but it upset her if any of the children were naughty. She taught the children to read and sew and Ada said she was best at making a neat patch or a darn. Some days she had to stay at home to wash or bake and missed school.

39 Children in this picture (20 boys and 19 girls) which was apparently taken at the same time as the picture on the previous page (page 35) where there were only 36 children.

April 6th was 'going up' day when former infants moved into the 'big room', as juniors. "Then it was stick and no play". Mr. Jowett liked to talk about his famous family. The children were never out of school on time as he always had to make up for lost time. When anyone was naughty, the stick would come hurling at them. Ada said that, 'it didn't matter where it hit us.' Sometimes they would have to stay in and write lines. Some of Ada's friends had to walk three miles to school - there was no transport in those days. Also, there were no school dinners and children just brought some jam and bread. When the school inspector came they had to be alert and answer questions quickly. In summary Ada felt she had a good education on the whole, but added that none of the children was sorry to leave when they reached the age of fourteen.

Religious Issues

The role of religion in education had continued to be controversial throughout the nineteenth-century but it would appear that Bishop Monkton was something of an outlier in this respect. The Church of England's objective was to get the maximum public subsidy while conceding the least possible control. On these issues the argument was between Anglicans and Roman Catholics on the one hand, and nonconformists and secularists on the other. The issue came to be one that also divided the political parties with the Church of England looking to the Conservatives for support, with nonconformists and radicals to the Liberals, who were still the second major political party in the early twentieth-century.

However, the managers of Bishop Monkton School formally adopted a policy in 1904 that, 'the religious instruction in school hours should till further notice be un-denominational,' and that 'the West Riding County Council syllabus of religious instruction be adopted.' This was not controversial for the villagers, given that they already had Wesleyan and Primitive Methodist chapels in addition to St. John's Anglican Church. Indeed, the vicar at the time, the Venerable William Danks, had felt able two years previously to write to 'The Times' on the matter. He wrote:- 'Half of the population of this Parish is nonconformist. Accordingly, we give them half the seats on the board. During the three years of this arrangement, we have had no difference of opinion on religious instruction. On the practical teaching of scripture and conduct to young children, the Free Protestant Churches and the Anglican Church would be puzzled to state their differences. Surely in all this debate there is a great deal of sound and fury which signifies nothing but political partisanship.'

The School's challenges

One way to get a picture of how the school was during this period is from the School's own records. The managers of Bishop Monkton School usually held formal meetings each month to discuss its affairs. Their chairman usually drafted the minutes himself and he was also designated the official 'correspondent' for communication with the West Riding County Council.

The managers' meetings dealt mostly with staffing matters, given their responsibility, subject to advice from the Council, for recruiting the teaching and domestic staff, and they considered the reports from the government inspectors on secular matters and the diocesan inspectors on non-curricular religious instruction. They also discussed and dealt with the upkeep of the school premises. A selection from the minutes of meetings in the first half of the twentieth-century gives a flavour of the issues facing the school.

July 1905: The Government Inspector reported about the Mixed Class: 'The School continues in good order but the Master has had over sixty children on his hands as a rule and the room used by the elder children has been too full for successful teaching.'

April 1908: At the request of the Council, the question of interesting parents in the education of their children was discussed, and Mr. Jowett was desired to send occasionally to the parents specimens of really good work done in school.

June 1909: A letter from the Council about medical inspection was read and the advantages of this inspection (commenced in 1907) were emphasised, and it was felt to be most important that the Medical Officer's orders should be carried out in all cases, whether as regards cleanliness, eyes, nose, ears, etc. The correspondent was asked to write to the Council suggesting that the managers were willing to assist in this work, and they should have the aid of Mrs. Summerfield, Miss Butterfield, and Miss Swales (if willing to serve) to visit the homes of children reported to be suffering in any way, and by sympathy and advice, encourage parents to do all in their power to remedy any physical defects of their children.

May 1910: The Chairman reminded Mr. Jowett that attention had been called to him, Mr. Jowett, that it was most important both for teachers, children, and parents that the School hours should not exceed those marked in the timetable, except in cases of punishment. Canon Reed advised Mr. Jowett not to talk to the children during lesson time of matters quite irrelevant to their work, e.g. people and events in the village – for, if this were done, there was no wonder the lessons would not be finished.

May 1910: The Chairman referred with pleasure to the good order he always found in the School, and to the attention given by the children to his Scripture Lessons from time to time.

Feb. 1915: The Correspondent interviewed all the managers respecting the Annual Report on Mrs. Jowett's work and the following was sent to the Council; 'The Managers consider that Mrs. Jowett's work is most satisfactory, especially when her age is taken into consideration - and the tone of the Infants' Department is excellent.'

March 1916: A letter was received from the Council suggesting the reduction of the staff to two teachers, thus setting free the uncertified assistant for service elsewhere. Resolved, that in the opinion of the Managers the proposed decrease of the teaching staff would be detrimental to the school, the present number of the teachers being necessary to efficiency.

Sept. 1916: Letters from the Board of Education and Council stated that when a head teacher's post becomes vacant it is the practice, if the average attendance does not exceed seventy-five, to advertise for a mistress at a commencing salary of £90.

Oct. 1916: Miss Helena Mary Shippam appointed Headteacher of Bishop Monkton National School at a salary of £95. Cordially agreed that the Chairman should write a letter addressed to Mr. and Mrs. Jowett, expressing the goodwill of the managers, and their best wishes, now that their long and honourable services to the school were about to terminate.

June 1918: Letter from the District Sub-Committee desiring the managers to submit proposals for the remainder of the long holidays up to the year ending January 31st, 1919, including the hay and corn harvest and potato picking.

March 1919: The managers regard Miss Shippam as a very efficient teacher, who tackles the problems of village education with enthusiasm and common sense.

1919 - The Infants

The Infants Teacher with her 21 pupils

1919 - The School

Miss Shippam (Head), Mabel Armitage, Harry Trueman, Reg Merrin, Harry Slater, Fred Armitage?, Lesley Prist, Eddie Slater, Sally Kench, Alice Kench
Freda Gledhill, Zena Gledhill, Mary Dixon, Dolly Curtis, Anne Trueman, Fanny Dovenor, Olive Lee, Vera Vasey, Muriel Thackwray, Ada Morland, Molly Wood, Madge Hymas
Eleanor Armitage, Annie Kench, Jessie Kench, Mary & Alice Curtis, Muriel Hall, Mary Hutchinson, Pop Armitage, Rene Merrin, Millie Armitage, Ettie Lee, Dorothy Slater
Jackie Thompson ??, ??, Fred Storry?, Harry Wood, Scout Hymas, Tony Curtis, Herbert Morland

Feb. 1921: The question of, 'banking up' the school fires for the evening was discussed; and the managers thought that such practice was unnecessary except (perhaps) in very severe weather. Such weather had not been experienced this Winter. They pointed out that one or other of the fires had often been burning hours after the close of afternoon school. The managers thought that there had thus been an extravagant use of fuel recently, and were of the opinion that due economy should be practised.

1922

Miss Shipham with some of the school's pupils

June 1922: Communication from County Hall suggested that the School should be efficiently conducted by Head Teacher and one Assistant instead of two as at present. Last year's average attendance was fifty-three and the number on the role on 7th April was fifty-seven. Agreed that the Correspondent should inform the County Council that, in view of the urgent need of economy, they did not feel able to press for a continuance of a staff of three teachers. After consideration of the needs of the school and the qualifications of the two assistants, it was agreed that the notice to leave should be given to Miss Eglin. The Managers sincerely regretted that they were compelled to part with a teacher so conscientious, reliable and loyal. (This was the period of the so-called 'Geddes Axe' and its severe cuts in public services in the aftermath of the First World War).

March 1923: The subject of carting the school coal and emptying the ashpits was then discussed. The chairman thought it would be well for the managers to express to Mr. Morrell their appreciation of his services and their regret that such services were not to be continued and to say that they were sorry that the Council Authority had acted upon insufficient knowledge of the conditions in our particular case.

March 1924: The government inspector's report was read. It contained both commendation and criticism. Reading, writing and arithmetic were said to be good. So too was drawing. But mental arithmetic, geography and history were rather weak. The progress of the infants was very satisfactory. The meeting agreed that the report was, on the whole, an excellent one.

March 1927: The report by the government inspector for 1926 was read, 'The managers have recently repaired and redecorated the premises and the work is carried on under much more pleasant conditions than formerly. The School is well conducted by a vigorous Head Mistress, whose personality has influenced the pupils. They are well behaved, industrious and ready to cooperate in the various lessons. The percentage of children in the Upper Standards is most creditable and the general standard of attainment of these children is praiseworthy. The reading in class needs attention and the points discussed in connexion with drawing should receive consideration.'

1925

School Trip to Fountains Abbey c. 1925

Late 1920's

Kathlene Hymas, Dorothy Johnson, Millie Armitage, Nell Kendrew, Dorothy Kendrew, Phyllis Waddington, Netta Hymas, Gladys Armitage, Nora Pybus,
Jimmy Kench, Harry Hymas, Stuart Renton, Henry Pybus, Billy Brown, Ken Morland, Billy Park, Edgar Judson, Alec Renton, Denis Hymas
??, Joyce Challoner

Aug. 1935: The managers then discussed the question of transferring the 11-plus children from Bishop Monkton School to a proposed senior school in Ripon. The Correspondent read certain correspondence from the Education Authority dealing with this matter. Afterwards the Managers thoroughly discussed the proposition from every point of view and unanimously rejected the proposal of the Education Authority.

Feb. 1936: The government inspector attended the meeting and fully explained the advantages of sending the 11+ age children to the proposed school to be built in Ripon. After much discussion, the managers agreed to the proposal.

June 1938: Various alterations to the School required by West Riding County Education Authority, as follows: central heating including cloakrooms, domestic hot water supply, additional lavatory bowls, conversion of offices to the water carriage system, modern glazed and flushed urinals.

1938 - The School

Oct. 1938: A letter read from the Education Authority concerning the alterations to the School, stating that they were unable to give a grant towards the work of renovating the School. This caused considerable surprise to those present and a discussion on the subject followed. Agreed that the matter of obtaining grants etc. be left in the hands of the Vicar.

Second World War

When the Second World War broke out in 1939, Bishop Monkton was impacted relatively little compared with other places. However, the village and the School were not untouched by the conflict. Three Monktoners were killed in action during the War. In April 1944 seven airmen died when a Halifax bomber crashed during a storm close to where the Village Hall now stands. Prisoners of war held in nearby camps were regularly seen in and around the village. The Army Bridging Camp on the edge of the village towards Roecliffe played a key role in the development and training associated with temporary bridges, including the famous 'Bailey Bridges' used in several Allied campaigns.

1939-1945 - Evacuees from Leeds

1939 Evacuees.

Muriel
(Dereek
behind left)

Some of the 600 or so children who were evacuated from Leeds to the Ripon area. Shown here, with a few village children, in the back playground of our school. Note that the wall dividing the playground was still in place.

The main impact on the School was the arrival at the beginning of the War of evacuees from Leeds and elsewhere. A poignant picture from 1939 shows them outside the School but little is known about them or how long they stayed here. An article from the 'Ripon Gazette' at the time talks about the outings they had enjoyed, including to Fountains Abbey and Ripon Cathedral. It also mentions that they had been to see the traditional hornblowing ceremony at 9 p.m. in Ripon Market Square, although a curfew later imposed on the children meant that they were not able to go there again.

The managers' minutes also record a couple of decisions taken by the School during wartime -

Dec. 1940: After some discussion and after viewing the premises it was decided to 'black out' the School; the blinds to be darkened and cardboard placed round the windows and the rollers repaired where necessary.

May 1941: The question of a ladder to reach the roof in case of incendiary bombs was discussed and it was agreed that the Correspondent write to the Divisional Clerk suggesting the provision of an extension ladder, and it could be used if necessary for fire-fighting in the village.

Bishop Monkton villagers during the Second World War - Wings for Victory

The Second World War also marks the limit of living memory still associated with the School. David Simpson, Margaret Simpson and Elizabeth Wilkinson all went to the School during or very soon after the War.

1944-45 - Wartime

School children in a wartime play held in the Old WI Hall.
David Simpson is on the right, standing between two nurses.

David Simpson is one of the oldest living ex-pupils and he attended the School from 1938 to 1944. He lived in the Limes, then a drapers shop and also at one time a Post Office run by his grandfather. His parents had also been to the School. He remembers the Headteacher, Miss Shippam and he remembers helping plant an oak tree outside the School near the beck. David remembers having to carry his gas mask around in a box and having to wear it in lessons. He remembers being in a school play during the War. He also has memories of going to the site of the Halifax bomber crash in 1944 and finding bullets in the wreckage.

Margaret Simpson was at the School from 1943 to 1946, from the age of five to eight when Miss Goss was the Headteacher. Margaret also remembers wearing gas masks in lessons which steamed up but which the children just had to get used to. She also remembers listening to the radio in school. She vividly remembers how the school was organised with the playground split with the area in front of the building for younger children aged five to eight, and the back section behind the school building for older children aged eight to eleven. These two small yards were not really big enough to play properly.

Classes were mixed with boys and girls together and mixed toilets in the back playground.

'The Old School' House - taken in 2024

Margaret Simpson (1943-46) and Clare Royds (1954-57) both former pupils

There were two classrooms split in the building by a light partition from front to back with the five to eight year olds on one side and the eight to eleven year olds on the other side. There was a fire or stove in each room. There were two teachers, one for juniors and one for seniors. Children were mostly from local farms or the paper mill.

There were no school meals – children went home for lunch. Punishment for bad behaviour often meant being hit with a ruler. To keep them healthy, children were fed cod liver oil from a 'green' spoon, but they were all fed this from the same spoon! A travelling dentist, an optician and the 'nit nurse' visited the school. The blacksmith next door cut their hair. Children were given time off in October for potato picking.

Post-War Memories

As the war came to an end, attention turned to new proposals, including the provision of school meals, which had been included in the Education Act of 1944, but which were not universally welcomed in Bishop Monkton. The managers' notes recorded the following-

Sept 1944: At a meeting of managers held on 7th September, it was resolved that the following reply be sent in answer to a letter from the Divisional Clerk about Provision of Meals: 'Knowing all the circumstances the managers consider that all the expenses involved in providing meals for the children of the above School are unnecessary and they oppose the scheme. They would however be pleased to have the scheme explained more fully by someone in authority.' On 8th December representatives of the Education Authority met the managers along with those from Burton Leonard and discussed and explained the scheme. It was agreed by managers of both schools that the scheme would be accepted under protest.

Elizabeth Wilkinson was at the School from 1946 to 1948 aged five to seven and her brother Colin Atkinson was also there from 1943 to 1948. She remembers the children's gas masks being pink. Elizabeth can remember school lunches, introduced after the 1944 Act, which were made by Ettie Lee up by Ings Lane and brought down to the School. She also remembers picking rosehips up Ings Lane which were made into rosehip syrup.

The managers' notes from the post-war period continued to reflect the practical issues which the School had to address, including the state of the toilets!

April 1951: A discussion took place on the possibilities of converting the earth lavatories to water closets. It was decided to get an estimate from Mr. Benson for the conversion. A discussion followed on the necessity of raising funds and it was proposed by the Vicar that the Wesleyan Chapel be invited to make a contribution. Mr. Benson proposed that a written appeal should be made to the village and Parish. The managers' meeting was followed by a meeting of parents and others interested in the welfare of the School and an appeal was drafted.

Nov. 1951: All the School managers were present and there was a large and representative company of the Parents' Association. Mr. Baxter reported that since the previous meeting the lavatories had been converted to the water carriage system and also that the internal decorations of the School had almost been completed.

The West Riding Authority would contribute 5/7th leaving approximately £33 for the managers to pay. On behalf of the Parents' Association, it was proposed that a cheque for £50 should be handed to the managers for the School account. This was done and the Vicar expressed on behalf of the managers their sincere appreciation for the gift and for the efforts that the Parents' Association had made and would continue to make.

1952

??, David Middlemist, Jimmy Wright, ??, John Kemp, ??, John Leighton, John Gray, ??
??, Susan Fryer, Alan Chisem, Rita Moore, Rosie Addyman, Geoffery Blaken, Yvonne Blaken, Michael Kemp, Sheila Sanderson

Several ex-pupils who were at the School in the 1950s and 1960s have vivid memories of their time there. **Alan Chisem** was there from 1950 to 1956 from the age of five to eleven.

His sister Joan Chisem was there from 1949 to 1955. They lived at Albion House Farm and have lived in the village a long time. They remember two classes divided by age into 'the small class and the big class.' Alan thinks that the playground at the back was divided by a wall, separating the two age groups, but that this was dismantled while he was there. Over the entrance door on the right hand side of the building, there was a school bell which was rung signalling playtime.

1954

Norman Hutchinson, ??, ??, Michael Lawson, Jimmy Wright, Colin Elliot, ??, Keith Sanderson, Christopher Thompson, ??, John Kemp, ??, **Mrs Walters**
??, Rosie Addyman, Susan Fryer, Judith Jackson, Carol Jennings, Christine Howard, Christine Jackson, Joan Chisem, Helen Channer, Eileen Hymas, ??
Sandra Riley, Vicky Hebden, Rita Moore, Jennifer Craggs, Julie Pallister, Lesley Howard, Lesley Hebden, Sheila Sanderson, Denise Hebden, Eileen Metcalfe, ??
Martin Usher, Geoffrey Blaken, Michael Kemp, Richard Waddington, ??

There was a coke boiler in the left hand room where the younger children were. In the right hand room was a Wendy house in the corner, used on one occasion to quieten down a naughty boy, who shook the Wendy house so hard he had a jug of water thrown over him! A large clock hung on the right hand wall in this room.

Lunch was delivered in canisters and before lunch the children ran up one side of the beck to the Masons Arms and down the other to work up an appetite. He remembers sponge pudding and custard for lunch. Punctuality was important and the rule was that they had to be there at 9 a.m. sharp. There was a 'kid catcher' who would come round to the house if a child wasn't attending to find out why they were not at school.

1956/7?

Keith Wood, John Leighton, Brian Metcalfe, Alan Chisem, Pip Channer, Michael Lawson, Jimmy Wright, Keith Hutchinson, The Green Twins, **Miss Willis**
Neil Piper, John Gray, Sandra Riley, Clare Royds, Lesley Howard, Susan Fryer, Rita Moore, Jennifer Craggs, Sybella Royds, Christopher Thompson, John Kemp
Susan Dobson, Penny Channer, Linda Bosomworth, Julia Pallister, Irene Metcalfe, Sheila Sanderson, ??, Valerie Sanderson, Susan Wilkinson, ? Metcalf
Graeme Kell, David Metcalfe, Richard Waddington, Geoffrey Blaken, Martin Usher, Geoffrey Graham, Stephen Blaken

Howard Morland started at the School aged four in 1957 and stayed until 1964. His parents William Kenneth Morland and Margaret Hilda Morland, tenant farmers at Low Farm, had also attended the School as did his grandparents and great-grandparents. Howard said the Headteacher, Miss Willis, was very highly thought of and encouraging. The other teacher was Miss Garner. He remembers organising a 'mock' wedding and getting chairs lined up in the playground for the 'congregation'. He also has memories of 'wars' between girls and boys. Miss Willis had a room at the back and sat at the window where she could keep an eye on the children. The School furniture consisted of tables in the classroom which were also used for lunch. There were fields at the Old Vicarage for sports and he has memories of children sitting round Miss Willis and being read stories.

1961 – Miss Willis and her Class on the cricket ground at Low Farm

Geoffrey Graham,   **Miss Doreen Willis**
Steven Blaken, Henry Royds, Susan Wilkinson, Howard Morland, ??, ??
Tony Waite, Jonathan Triscott, Yvonne Blaken, Robert Steele, Valerie Sanderson, Philip Steele

There were no uniforms and punishment was either a ruler, being kept back or possible caning. There were regular weekly visits from Rev. Ibbotson for prayers and a song was sung by the children at the end of every day before leaving for home. Lessons included Maths and English with regular testing both verbal and written, and there were also some creative lessons - cookery, art, bible studies, woodwork. He made boats to race and won an award for writing stories. Children listened to the radio programme 'Singing Together' and sang some English folk songs. Mrs. Burnard from Well Farm next door had some of the children round to watch BBC Schools programmes on television. School trips took place once a year to places such as Brimham Rocks and How Stean Gorge.

Late 1960's? - Annual Brimham Rocks Trip

Miss Willis, older pupils plus staff and 'helpers' on a trip to Brimham Rocks

Clare Royds started at the School aged eight in 1954 when Mrs. Walters was the Headteacher. Miss Garner was the infant teacher who always wore white socks. Clare remembers that the children had to share books and that everyone helped each other. Even though the playground was small, they managed to play rounders there and the boys had motor tyres to roll around in. Clare remembers a school outing to Scarborough by bus and being given oranges and chocolate to eat.

Clare remembers Miss Willis first coming to the School for an interview and to spend some time in the village before starting as Head. She recalls that petrol rationing had been reintroduced because of the Suez Crisis, so Miss Willis lodged with Miss Hodgson near the School. Later, when she went back to her own home in Follifoot, Miss Willis bought a dog called Chummy for Miss Hodgson. The dog was very popular with the children. Clare said that the School taught her good manners, how to behave and to work hard. The teachers were very good and mainly concentrated on Maths and English. She remembers lots of spelling tests!

On the Move

By the time Clare was a pupil and when Doreen Willis became Headteacher in 1956, the need for more space and the idea of moving to a new site was already being discussed. In fact, the discussion had started at the end of the Second World War. In 1947 the School managers were involved in discussions about a 'West Riding Development Plan' which had suggested a new school on a new site in Bishop Monkton, something they opposed.

In 1952 a crucial decision was taken which would define the future of the School and which would eventually lead to the move to a new site. Whilst remaining a Church of England School, it became a 'Controlled School' which meant that the County

Council had much more say in its running and which opened up potential funding for development. Extracts from the managers' log describe what happened:-

May 1952: A letter was read from the Ripon Diocesan Board of Control asking for consideration as to whether the School should become 'Aided' or 'Controlled.' The cost to the Church if 'Aided' status is desired would be £6,505. It was generally agreed that there was no possibility of raising that amount, but the managers who were available were asked to attend a meeting to be held by the Ripon Diocesan Council to obtain as much information on the subject as possible.

June 1952: Mr. Benson, Mr. Blaker and Mr. Baxter gave a report of the meeting which had been held in the Cathedral Library for consideration of 'Aided or Controlled' status of the School. After a full discussion it was agreed that application should be made to the West Riding Education Authority for 'Controlled' status.

However, it was to be more than a decade before the village got a new site for its school, The managers' minutes of 22nd May 1956 record the following:-

'There followed a discussion on the County Development Plan for a new school building. The unanimous opinion of the managers was that they did not approve the site suggested for the new school building on the grounds of (a) that the land was often flooded in winter time, (b) the expense involved in preparing the site, and (c) that a better alternative is to develop the site behind the existing School building.'

It is thought that the site originally proposed for the new school was the field opposite the Mechanics' on Boroughbridge Road next to Hall Farm – a piece of land which has in more recent times been rejected by planners as a possible site for housing development. However, it was clearly the case that option (c) was eventually chosen but it was to take another decade for the Council to find the money to turn the vision into reality. It was eventually included in the West Riding's Minor Building Plan of 1967/68 and the School was built by Alvic Construction (Northern) Ltd. of Bradford. The managers' log of 5th November, 1970 recorded that:-

'Phase 1 of the new Bishop Monkton C.E. School was formally taken over from the contractors. The decision to build the School was in the 1967/68 Minor Building Plan. 127 sq.yds of the new school site was sold to Mr. John Moon, Bridgend Cottage for the extension of his garden. There were seventy-two children on the roll, sixty-six have a school dinner.'

The School was all set to move into a new era.

1968

The New School Plan - 1970

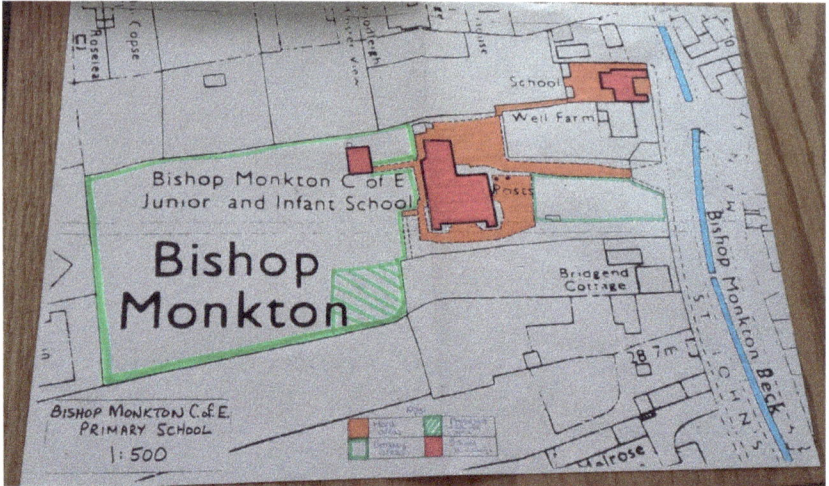

Late 1960's - School site development (far right) and The Masons Arms and
Melrose Farmhouse (central) before Melrose road building

CHAPTER THREE – 1971 – 2025
Developing on a new site into the twenty-first century

Headteachers

1956-1991 Miss Doreen Willis

1991-1995 Peter Brunt

1995-2009 Christine Duffield

2009 – 2025 Sally Cowling

Key Dates

1967 – Plowden Report – set out a 'child-centred' policy for teaching in primary schools' – a policy loved by progressives but loathed by many traditionalists.

1980 Education Act – established parent governors and gave more power to parents, also abolished free school milk.

1988 Education Act – established the National Curriculum.

2020-22 Major disruption to schools during the Covid Pandemic.

For almost thirty years after 1971, Bishop Monkton School was a dual site school with the original building still used and linked by a passageway to the new site. At the turn of the century, the new site was expanded and the old site sold off to become a private house. For the half-century since the 1970s, apart from a short period in the early 1990s, the School has been run by three long-serving headteachers, one of whom was very long-serving.

The Doreen Willis Years (1956-1991)

More than thirty years after her retirement, many people in Bishop Monkton still recall Doreen Willis, Headteacher from 1956 to 1991, with great affection. Miss Willis kept a diary of her time at the School which she described as "a very happy thirty five years". Extracts from her diary, as well as articles from local papers, give an insight into the life of the School, starting with the move which took place in 1970/71.

Miss Willis

Dec. 1970: Great excitement today - moving day had finally arrived. Some furniture had been delivered – chairs, but no tables, cupboards or storage lockers. The children brought suitcases and boxes. Everyone worked extremely hard, excitedly carrying books and equipment from the old school to the new building. After the cramped conditions, the space and light were appreciated by everyone. The sun shines into the classroom and hall.

Jan. 1971: During this month we have had both hilarious and frustrating times. Fifty teak top tables (senior size) were delivered and left in the playground. Eventually they had to be carried inside where they filled all available space. Chairs delivered were infant size - the children decided the floor was the place to work! Very strong representations were made to the suppliers and replacements were promised.

March 1971: Managers' meeting, Mrs. Worth appointed - a second infant class to be formed after Easter.

July 1971: Instead of an official opening for the school we have decided to celebrate this event with a school project connected with village life in Victorian times. The exhibition was open for three days and was visited by many of the villagers and former pupils. We thought it had been an interesting and successful time.

Sept. 1971: Fourth-year Juniors visited London accompanied by Miss Willis, Mrs. Blackett and Mrs. Patterson - a very successful visit.

Feb. 1972: Managers' meeting. It was reported that the Divisional Architect has suggested that the existing boiler which heats the Old School should be replaced by an oil-fired system and installed in the outside stone buildings.

July 1972: Miss Shippam, former Headteacher, visited the school and told the children what school life was like earlier in the century. Everyone was interested, especially when she told them about the beck overflowing and flooding the school - a boat was used to take the children home. One day a cow rushed into the school!

July 1973: All the School went to Brimham Rocks for a picnic and to pick (and eat) bilberries.

Nov 1973: Complained to the Council about the low temperature in the classrooms. The East classroom is the colder.

On 20th December 1974, the 'Ripon Gazette' reported that all the children in the Junior School took part in a performance of 'A Christmas Carol'.

May 1976: Miss J. Morley sent a letter of complaint about footballs being sent into her garden. She would like the goalposts to be positioned across the field. This is not possible. Mrs. J. Moon is complaining about the same problem.

July 1976: All the School went to Sandsend. Some children walked to Whitby and looked around the docks and fishing boats. Other children went along the cliff walk for several miles. The infants played on the beach and enjoyed hunting for fossils and in the rock pools.

Dec.1979: 'Christmas Afternoon' which involved children from Mrs. Blackett's, Mrs. Hardacre's, Miss Roper's and Mrs. Pearson's classes. This was extremely enjoyable. Musical items around Christmas songs - Frosty the Snowman, Rudolf and Jingle Bells. In the evening the children from Mrs. Rothery's and Miss Willis's performed 'A Medieval Christmas'. This year the number of seats for the evening performances had to be regulated. Admission was by ticket only, obtainable in advance. The numbers were more manageable but excluded older people who had always supported the School in the past - they were very disappointed.

1980's

The Old School, still in use showing its back yard (dividing wall gone) and outside toilet block

In 1982, the 'Ripon Gazette' reported on an egg rolling competition organised and judged by Miss Willis in the run-up to the Easter holidays.

Feb.1983: A meeting for parents to consider the future of financing swimming for the children. The School can no longer charge for this activity. The meeting was extremely well attended with each family in the School being represented. Parents were unanimous that swimming should continue and that they would all pay 'voluntary contributions'.

In January 1986, the 'Ripon Gazette' reported that Bishop Monkton School had become the first in North Yorkshire to install solar panels. This followed a temporary pilot scheme reported by the paper in 1979.

And on 9th March 1990, the paper reported that members of 51 Squadron had found time in their busy training schedule to deliver a tree trunk to the School to be a new piece of playground equipment.

In April 1993, the Friends of Bishop Monkton School organised a 'mobile ice rink' for children and parents to enjoy in the W.I. Hall in the village.

And in February 1997, the 'Ripon Gazette' mentioned that a jumble sale was to be held on 8th March in Bishop Monkton W.I. Hall to raise funds for a memorial bench for Doreen Willis who had died a short time before, only a few years after her retirement as Head.

Sue Brown, who lived in Mouse Cottage, was a pupil from 1966 to 1972 during the years of the move to the new site. The Vicar was Rev. Ibbotson who visited the school regularly. Sue attended Sunday School and was one of the first girls to sing in the church choir.

Lessons were in a portacabin beyond the old school playground wall, which was reached by going through a snicket in the wall and they also played in the field behind the portacabin. She remembers milk in small bottles, orange juice and malt extract (Virrol).

Punishment for talking or not doing homework would involve being told to stand in the cloakroom or staying behind to do lines.

Since 2006 Sue has been back at the School as a dinner lady. She says the quality of meals has improved beyond recognition since she was a pupil. Meals are more balanced and healthier, with everything being made on the premises including bread.

Food is a recurrent theme! **Florence Bowes** worked in the new school starting in 1977 as a kitchen assistant, when Mrs. Lawtry was the Cook, before taking over as the Cook herself in 1983 and continuing until 1996. All four of her own children attended the school. Food was provided by YPO (Yorkshire Purchasing Organisation) and Gilmour Foods. 120 lunches were cooked each day and the meals cooked were generally what the children liked - fish fingers, sausages, mince, beans, potatoes and veg. Puddings were chocolate crunch, steam puddings, jam roly-poly and custard, to name a few.

Lunch was from 12 to 1 p.m. and eaten in the hall, generally eight on a table and approximately fifteen tables. Hot food was put into rectangular food tins called 'Coffins', placed on the tables and served out by dinner ladies. The children drank water. The canteen was scrubbed out every Friday and all paperwork was done on Fridays. NYCC set out menus and all meals had to be carried out as specified. These changes were intended to make healthier meals and included more fruit.

Florence also recalls that, during Miss Willis's time as Head, any naughty children ate their meals at her table, where, while they were waiting for their food, they were made to recite their times tables!

1960's - Lunch Time

Sarah Worthington, who has been the School's Office Manager since 2008, was a pupil from 1977 to 1983. Sarah started in the old school in 1977 for two years until 1979 taught by Mrs. Blackett, then in the portacabin for one year, and then transferred to the new school from 1981 to 1983. There were 125 pupils in the school at that point. Next door to the school was Forge Garage, which Sarah's parents owned and ran, and Sarah lived next door to this, at Forge Cottage and so went home for lunch. For most pupils, lunch was taken in the new school along the path from the old school. The school bell, which used to hang outside the junior entrance door of the old school, is now outside the main entrance door to the current building.

Sarah recalls:- "Discipline was either the ruler, slipper or a smack but Miss Willis was very well respected and very kind, and, in the main, children knew their boundaries. Play was on a climbing frame in the 'back field' and egg rolling took place at Ashbrook Farm at Easter. Easter, Christmas and Harvest Festival were always celebrated in the church, and Rev. Ibbotson was a frequent visitor to the school. Trips were to Brimham Rocks where they could pick bilberries and often came back with blue faces."

During the 1980s, and ever since, the School has increasingly attracted children from outside the village, partly because of its good reputation, falling numbers of young children in Bishop Monkton and the lack of a school in many neighbouring villages. Another change, after the Education Act of 1980, has been the greater involvement of parents in the School with parent governors appointed and parent helpers coming into the School more often.

Christine Feeny worked as a parent helper from 1987 to 1990. She taught Craft subjects on Monday afternoons to children aged eight to eleven in groups of five or six children. Christine taught simple needlework like cross stitching and machine sewing. Children rotated through the groups.

In 1976, Miss Willis accepted two children in the village with Special Needs into the School. One of them was Christine's daughter Kate, who had Downs Syndrome, and another boy. They were taught in the old school by Mrs. Noblett for three hours each morning. At this point there was no legal requirement on schools to provide for children with special needs.

1978 - Mrs Blackett's (reception) Class

Mrs Blackett
Damian Quinn, David Howell, Nicholas Crouch, Philip Hare, Neil Watson, Richard Sharman
Jayne Lodge, Lucy Wallace, Melonie Heap, Jeanette Smith, SallyAnn Birchall, Julie Waldron
Neil McKeone, Edward Bolton, William Richardson, Sarah Knowles, David Shand, Thomas Wilson
Corrie Swope, Ross Minett, Clifford Blades, Paul Heap, Matthew Barnett, Matthew Barker

Carole Minett also worked at the School as a parent helper from 1987 to 1990. She taught hobbies to the older children aged nine to eleven. Carole had sewing machines and taught both boys and girls machine sewing and making simple things like aprons and mats. She remembers Mr. Dickinson who had a smallholding at Springfield House in Mains Lane where he had an orchard and a hand-pumped drinking water well. Mrs. Blackett did a yearly nature walk to his place, where children learnt about and sampled the produce there, including a glass of well water. Mr. D, as he was known, organised a Christmas goody bag consisting of a KitKat and an apple from his orchard for each child in the School.

1981 Miss Willis's (top) Class

??, Simon Dickinson, Nicholas Roome, Ashley Horner, William Richardson, ??, Paul Birchall, Mark Cuthbert
Lisa Nicholson, Catherine Osborne, Sarah Nicholson, Sarah Miller, **Miss Doreen Willis**
??, Lisla Wallace, Kirsty Minett, Claire Sharman, Rachel Barker, Lindsay Sommerville, Louise Walmsley

1982 Mrs Rothery's Class

Mrs Rothery, Matthew Barker, Glen Anderson, Nicholas Dingwall, Damian Quinn, Edward Bolton, Paul Heap
Nicky Howard,Charles Feeny,Daniel Cooke,Jane Lodge,Emma Jones,Lisa Houseman,Paul Hemming,Karl Wright,Nicholas Crouch,Simon Wright,Ross Minett
Chris Jones, Nicola Holmes, Sarah Sowerby, Helen Wilson, Sarah Posselthwaite, Victoria Lee, Lizabeth Nicholson, Gary Wilks, Stuart Hague

Jen Barker was a parent governor from the early 1980s until the early 1990s when she also became Chair of the Governors. In those days, governors met once a term in the new school and were involved in new staff interviews. Children numbers had expanded substantially in the 1970s to 144 as a result of the building of Melrose and Meadowcroft houses. The introduction of the National Curriculum resulted in science subjects being introduced in addition to Maths and English, and necessitated the re-training of teachers.

Jen returned as a Governor in 2020 when more parent involvement was required and in specific areas. Standards were stricter and there was a requirement to make sure the curriculum was adhered to. By this time the Board of Governors had a broader spectrum of members including some from the Council.

1982 Middle Class

Edward Bolton, Damian Quinn, Nicholas Dingwall, Ross Minett, Paul Heap, ??
Nicholas Crouch, Matthew Barker, Glen Anderson, ??, Paul Hemmings, ??, Gary Wilks
Lisa Houseman, Emma Jones, Jane Lodge, Lizabeth Nicholson, ??, SallyAnn Birchall

1984 Miss Roper's Infants Class

1984 Mr Whiteley's (senior) Class

??, Edward Bolton, ??, Damian Quinn, Matthew Barker, **Mr Whiteley**
Gary Wilks, ??, Ross Minett, Jane Lodge, SallyAnn Birchall, Paul Hemmings, ??, Paul Heap
??, ??, ??, Emma Jones, ??

1985 Christmas

Glen Turner, ??, Charley Smithson, ??, Samantha Williamson, Steve ?, Ryan Goodman, Laura Short, Erika Short
??, Mark Hopper, Jamie Lee, Vicky McBride, Marcus Potts?, Nicholas Craigie, ??, Michael Roome, Ian Taylor, Mark Lodge, Mathew Blaken, ??
David Jones, ??, Simon Jones, ??, Claire Houseman, ??, Rowena Richardson, Richard Mullens, Richard Howell, ??, Adam Stewart, Daniel Wigby, Nicholas Jones
Luke Streets, Emily Feist, Isobel Blaken, Ben Newsome, ??, ??, ??, ??, Melanie Chisem, Sarah Craigie, Alex Minett, Rebecca Hargreaves, Ian Walters, ??, ??, ??, ??,
John Errington, ,??, ??, ??   Matthew Potts
??,Charlotte Blaken, ??, ??, ??,??, Julie Claphan, Victoria Roberts, ??, ??, Kerry Claphan, ??, Helen Graham, ??, Joanna Moore

The Christine Duffield Years (1995-2009)

The Headteacher's log was no longer being kept up by the time Christine Duffield took up her post, but when she retired she did record her parting thoughts in the log's closing pages.

"During the past fourteen years the School has changed and developed in many ways. Gone are the metal climbing frames that once stood in the middle of the playground. In their place is a timber, much enjoyed agility trail on the grass and an extended playground complete with various markings to enhance play. A wildlife area has been created on the back field in one corner. This is much loved by the children, especially when they get the chance to get a dip in the large pond it encloses. In the summer it is teeming with life and also frequented by the village ducks.

"The portacabin classroom no longer belongs to the School, having been sold to Puddleducks Pre-School in 2004. Having them on site has added to the attraction of the School, especially in the last two years under the excellent leadership of Angela Oldershaw (playleader) and Fiona Bailey (chairperson). Also gone is 'The Old School' which was sold for development and is now a private residence. In 1999 we celebrated the 150th year of the School - The Old School opened in 1849. So we were sad to part with a bit of our history, but excited about the opportunities the sale created. The closure of that part of the School was marked by a study of the School's past and an open day and a Victorian exhibition. This was much enjoyed by past pupils, who came to visit and reminisce.

"A new extension, at the rear of the main school built in 2004, has replaced the 'Old School' classroom and the portacabin.

2004 Major Extension at the rear

"All classes are housed under one roof now and the Headteacher has a room too! The extension was built as a 'Design and Build' project which meant that the Governors and I were able to ensure we got exactly what we wanted from the project - spacious, modern classrooms with good ICT facilities, good storage and easy access to the classrooms. It certainly enhanced the School and saw the School move to higher all-round successes.

The School – Aerial View from the Rear showing the 2004 Extension

Note that the old school was vacated and converted into a private residence with the outhouse buildings at the rear removed and a pitched roof conservatory added to the building. This photo was taken around 2010.

"The curriculum has changed over the years with embedding the National Curriculum, and introducing a Literacy and Numerary Strategy. During this period we have continued to offer a rich and relevant curriculum at Bishop Monkton C.E. School at the same time as being committed to high standards in literacy and numeracy. The curriculum has expanded to include many aspects reflecting society today - ICT, global awareness, fair trade, climate change, multi-cultural, multi-faith understanding, sustainable development, finance education and Sound Emotional Aspects of Learning (SEAL).

"At the same time the emphasis has moved from the quality of teaching to the quality of learning. Assessment for Learning (AfL) and Assessing Pupil Progress all encourage learners to take ownership of their learning and to build on the feedback given by teachers. The 'learning' environment is an important aspect of a school with 'learning walls' replacing some of the walls previously given to 'display'. Staff now have PPA (Planning, Preparation, and Assessment) time and to some extent the workforce has been modernised. There are now more teaching assistants in school to support the focus on learning and to help every child achieve their best."

Some of the most vivid and detailed memories of the School in the second half of the twentieth-century come from **Sue Roome** who was a teacher here from 1970 to 2009. She was later Chair of Governors. Sue's recollections make fascinating reading:-

"When I started teaching, the children were all keen to learn and were motivated. This continued throughout my time there, but in the latter years, during the late 1990's onwards, we had several disruptive children who took a lot of time from the teachers and challenged the learning of the children. The Education Authority decided that these children would be better learning in an ordinary school environment which made it difficult for teaching staff and assistants. I only ever had a teaching assistant when I moved into the new school, and never had any help until then, so I always enlisted the parent helpers who were invaluable.

1992

Tom Everingham?, Jennifer Handley, Ben Pridmore, Jamie Hassell, Christopher Mullens, Helen Graham
Kerry Clapham, Thomas Shoesmith, Neil Blaken, Dominic Gregson, **Mrs Roome**, Sarah Allen, Alex Payne, David Holmes
Stephanie Cop, Luke Streets, Ben Harrison, Faye Higgins, Claire Wood, Emily Feist
James Cross, David Roberts, ??, Sam Newsome

"We began to take students from York St John latterly and this was helpful. I remember one boy standing up and telling the student teacher that he was spelling a word wrongly. The rest of the class were horrified!

"Lessons changed with the onset of the National Curriculum as we had to teach to government specifications. They were still made interesting but every detail of planning needed to be written down. I always had a science morning every Friday which involved experiments, recording findings, investigations and results. All aspects of science were covered which also included English, Maths, Art and Social Skills required for working in a group. The ability to plan, do the experiment, record and analyse the results were all part of the process. It took the joy and spontaneity out of teaching.

1994

Sean Coleman, Matthew Potts, **Mrs Roome**, Kris Burtwistle, Robert Myers
Jason Holmes, Sebastian Graham, Richard Mullens, Jonathan Lynn, Jamie Steele
Joanne Moore, Harriet Leach, Newton Hassell, Jamie Ebbage
Eleanor Garnett, Emily Feist, Charlotte Wilson

"Art afternoons, which I had every Tuesday afternoon, were fantastic because I usually had many parent helpers. We did art, technology and baking which resulted in a project combining all three. We drew every house along the street where the school was, each child chose a house to draw in black and white and also painted the house. Then each child translated these pictures into a clay model, which was then fired and painted, and then reassembled the line of houses as seen in the street.

"When Miss Willis was there, children did not wear uniforms and could come dressed in any clothes as long as they were tidy and clean. When Peter Brunt took over they all had a school top to wear, which was a T-shirt for sport and a jumper with the school logo on. This progressed to full uniform when Chris Duffield was Head which was better especially on school trips when the children were easily identifiable.

"When Miss Willis was Head, misdemeanours were punished by a ruler over the knuckles or the slipper, which was only carried out by her. Class discipline was good generally at this time. When Peter Brunt took over, children were made to stand outside the Head's door or do lines during playtime.

1996

Mrs Roome, Robert Myers, Jamie Ebbage, Alexandra Roberts, Jason Holmes, Kris Burtwistle, (student teacher)
Newton Hassell, Damien Allen, Holly Byres, Harriet Leach, Jonathan Lynn, Charlotte Wilson, Robin Clarke, ??
Richard Mullens, Rachel Cross, ??, Eleanor Garnett, Hazel Cottrell, Emily Wilson, Harriet Gallen, Erin Warden, Hannah Tyreman
Timothy Feist, Rachel Steele, James Tyreman, William Bainbridge, Max Crouch.

"When I was teaching in the old school, there were some very old computers and printers for the older children, but they were used quite successfully. When we transferred to the new school, we had a bank of up to date computers along one side of the classroom, all classrooms had computers then which were used a lot. There was also a trolley of laptops shared by the top two classes which were not always reliable, particularly if not plugged in to recharge overnight.

1994 - Netball Team

Mrs Roome
Eleanor Garnett, Charlotte Wilson, Stephanie Cop, Jonathan Lynn, Joanne Moore, Emily Feist
Helen Graham, Sarah Allen, Claire Wood, Alex Payne, Kerry Clapham

"We always had a football and netball team which played against local schools. When the government put forward a new initiative to do more sport, we undertook to do all kinds of sport. Another teacher, **Mandy Coupland**, was in charge of arranging 'taster sessions' in many sports such as tennis, basketball, rugby (we had a link with Bradford Bulls where a player came to coach the children). They took part in cross-country competitions each year and there were Kwik cricket matches with local schools. Swimming lessons were also on the agenda, and, in Miss Willis's time, we took children weekly to Ripon Spa Baths. At that time, no child left school without being able to swim. Later, to cut down costs, only certain classes went each term.

2000 Reception Class

Names – unfortunately few, just Bryn May (Minett) and Jonathan Venables, the 2nd and 3rd left on the front row

"In the early years, children didn't travel far from the village, and during Miss Willis's time they had two annual trips, one to Brimham Rocks and the other to Marske by the Sea.

In later years, trips were organised around topics the children were studying, for example Vikings would lead to a visit to the Jorvik Centre and workshops and a Viking lunch.

2003 Pond dipping in the school pond

2003 Robinwood - one of the many outdoor and indoor activities

"Trips to London for the older children were always a yearly highlight and I took two classes to London for the day, doing a circuit starting at the British Museum, St Pauls, the Tower of London, Houses of Parliament, Downing St, Buckingham Palace then picnicking in St. James's Park before coming home. Other times it included the Millennium Dome, Museum of London and Hyde Park. Trips were filled with laughter and enjoyment including two boys who jumped on the tube train when the doors closed and they sped off leaving the rest of us behind. Fortunately they had all been taught what to do in this situation and we were all reunited at the next station.

"The 'Just Linking' project with Leeds Development Education Centre aimed to link rural primary schools with large multicultural schools in Leeds. Our link was with Brudenell Primary in Leeds, where we made several exchange visits. We celebrated the different cultures through art, dance and literacy and explored the differences of environment and religion and ethnicity. On one exchange they all took a walk from the school to the canal with a picnic lunch. As they walked past the chicken farm, the city children didn't know what they were and were frightened because they had no experience of farms and country life, and chicken for them came from a supermarket. Likewise when they passed a cow in the field. After the picnic at the lock they asked when the taxi was coming to pick them up – it was a long walk back!"

2004 - Victorian Day

2004 - Victorian Day - in the old schholroom

2005 - Linking with a Leeds School

The Sally Cowling Years (2009 to date)

Likewise during the tenure of the current Headteacher, Sally Cowling, there was no requirement to keep a log or a diary. However, here are her reflections on what she describes as a 'small village school with a big heart.'

"My first visit to BM was as a prospective headteacher, taking a tour of the site. There were ducklings on the wildlife pond, daffodils up the drive, and the sunshine was glistening on the beck. What was not to love about the School? On appointment, there were around fifty-eight children on role in two and a half classes – three in the morning, reducing to two in the afternoon when Mrs.

Roome took all of KS2 (Juniors) in the hall. Classes were named 1, 2 and 3. My first term as Head involved appointing a new teacher to replace Mrs. Roome who had been at the School for her entire teaching career of thirty-nine years - a tough act to follow but we managed to appoint a male teacher, which I felt was important, amongst our all-female staff.

"During my time as Head, the most significant changes have been in our growth - in numbers, buildings, staffing and in the age range of the children. The School opened a nursery in April 2016, which started with thirteen children on roll in a carefully created space between two classrooms before moving into the portacabin that had originally been a classroom in the 1970's. This has now evolved into a purpose-built nursery building (built December 2024) which offers provision for children from two years old and currently has thirty-five children on roll.

"In 2010, a new front entrance was built and the access to the hall rearranged to align with the new entrance. At the front of the entrance, we put up the old school bell (originally erected in 1887) on the outside wall. Three times a day this historic bell still calls the children into the classroom – a wonderful reminder of the school's history. A window was put in the office so that visibility on to the front playground improved. The new entrance provided additional space as well as making the staff room and storerooms less visible to parents. It also created a better first impression for visitors. Over time, the library moved in to the front entrance, which then allowed that space to be used as additional teaching space.

"Our numbers have steadily grown over this time, with 143 children now on roll in both school and nursery (110 in primary). The addition of the nursery has helped growth along with the before and after school club which was established in September 2008. Classes are now named after birds and the traditional "coloured" team houses are now named after the Yorkshire Dales.

"Safeguarding has become more important and rightly so. This has resulted in higher fencing to our school site, identity badges, locks on doors and increased awareness of all staff as well as the draining of the pond to make more of a woodland area.

2012 - At the Queen's Diamond Jubilee there was a countrywide plan to plant several million trees, and the Woodland Trust were supplying bundles of saplings. In March 2012, with the help of all of the children in the village school, we planted 100 trees in two corners of the QEII Playing Fields.

"Our enrichment activities have expanded from a residential two nights away at Robin Wood, to three nights abroad to Le Touquet, France for Year Five, and four nights away at East Barnby, Whitby for Year Six. We have a yearly trip for the whole school to the pantomime and in 2025 we have launched BM 50 – 50 activities which we want children to complete before they leave at the end of Year Six. All fifty activities promote social, moral, spiritual and cultural experiences for children.

"The enjoyment I have had as a Head over the years has been immeasurable. Times spent in the classroom teaching (usually Religious Education (RE) or Personal, Social, Health Education (PSHE)) are my favourites, but whole school walks, visits to Yorkshire Sculpture Park, residentials abroad, sharing in our Celebration Assemblies and spending time talking to the children are just as worthwhile.

"However, there was a period in my Headship when leading the School each day was a challenge. March 2020 brought the first school closure due to Covid. The first we knew that schools were going to close was listening to Boris Johnson's bulletin with the rest of the nation. Immediately plans had to be put in place to ensure we could deliver remote learning. March to June 2020 in School was a strange place with only a handful of vulnerable children still being educated on site.

"I remember delivering assemblies from an echoing school hall – filming myself giving out virtual awards, celebrating achievements and generally trying to keep a sense of community going for us all. Even PE lessons were delivered remotely with me demonstrating skills on the field! A bizarre, unique time in the history of our School

– the daily news updating us with the latest statistics of cases. Running the School became an even bigger challenge when some children were allowed back in but had to be kept separate from one another, in 'bubbles'. The daily worry of keeping everyone safe cannot be underestimated – these were dark, difficult times.

"Although much of our school day is different to the curriculum content of the 1900s, timeless activities still continue, such as nature walks up Ings Lane to spot the signs of spring, racing boats on the beck, celebrating in St John's church with the local vicar, using the field to re-enact historical battles or for enjoying sports day. Attendance now though is compulsory – absences for haymaking or brambling would certainly be unauthorised!

2022 - Mothering Sunday - class card making

"Education is always a journey and over my time as Head, there have been several iterations of curriculum content, assessment and inspection frameworks. These changes, along with a yearly new intake of pupils, keeps every year fresh and exciting. There are never two days the same and my plan for the day may quickly be side-lined when something else needs addressing. The cyclical nature of the school calendar, with its blend of familiar traditions and evolving contributions from both children and staff, creates a dynamic and fresh atmosphere around key Christian festivals like Harvest, Christmas, and Easter. As a result, each new school year feels renewed and vibrant, fostering a sense of engagement and excitement within the school community. It is both the familiarity and the new that provides daily joy for me as the Headteacher."

CHAPTER FOUR – THE MECHANICS' INSTITUTION
Victorian Self-improvement for Adults

1950's & 60's - Mechanics Institution

Since the turn of the current century, it has been a house but, for 150 years before that from 1849 to 1999, it was the Mechanics' Institution, a rare example in such a small place of one of the great educational initiatives from the Victorian age. Had it not been for the vision of John Butterfield, Bishop Monkton would probably never have had one. Mechanics' Institutions, born out of Victorian ideals of self-improvement of the working classes, were generally to be found in cities and large towns. However, Butterfield, who had seen the benefits they could bring in Keighley where he had lived before moving to Bishop Monkton in 1846, decided that it was just what the village needed.

Unitarians and Quakers had a major role in the birth of Mechanics' Institutions. The seeds of adult education in England were sown by Dr. George Birkbeck when he took his ideas south from Glasgow to London and founded the first Mechanics' Institution there in November 1823. His idea spread first to Manchester and Newcastle and then on across the industrial towns of the Midlands and the North. By the peak in the 1850s, nearly 700 Institutions had opened. Among them Keighley, where John Bradley, a local painter, and three friends founded its Institution in 1825. It was such a success that, within ten years, it had moved into its own premises and by 1870 had built a grand hall that justified a ceremonial opening by the Duke of Devonshire. The Keighley Institution thus grew up alongside John Butterfield and inspired him.

The nineteenth-century witnessed great industrial growth in the North of England. Ever increasing numbers of entrepreneurs, managers and work people were needed to fuel this vast expansion of businesses and the new technologies essential to their success, but the starting point was one of rudimentary education and low literacy. The way forward could only come from personal ambition by way of self-improvement. The emerging professional classes paved the way by developing new institutions to build and share the new knowledge and skills needed to manage innovative businesses and to satisfy the needs of ever larger communities.

Business and community leaders could clearly see the benefits flowing from educating the artisan classes, but they also understood that the impetus needed to come from within

Institutes' memberships if they were to flourish, and accordingly the hope was that Institutes should be self-governed and self-funded, even if initial help in finding premises might need to be offered. The constitution of one Institution said the objective was 'to enable mechanics and artisans, of whatever trade they may be, to become acquainted with such branches of science as are of practical application in the exercise of that trade, that they may possess a more thorough knowledge of their business and acquire a greater degree of skill in the practice of it.'

When John Butterfield moved to Bishop Monkton, he became a business partner at the Paper Mill. He was a churchman, a Liberal of the old tradition and admirer of Gladstone and Charles Dickens as an author. He was a townsman by birth but was conscious that Bishop Monkton lacked a social community centre. He had been fortunate in life and wanted to give something back to the village. The land for the Mechanics', near the ford over the beck, was sold by Frederick Greenwood Esq. and was purchased by Butterfield and ten of his neighbours. They were John Greenwood Esq. MP; The Rev. Robert Poole; John Batty, Farmer; John Chambers, Builder; George Ward, Cordwainer; Joseph Cowling, Builder; William Coates, Builder; George Heath, Farmer; Richard Wall, Farmer and Benjamin Chambers, Mason.

On the 21st November 1859, Bishop Monkton's Mechanics' Institution opened with a grand fanfare. An early prospectus written by Butterfield proclaimed, "Young men of Yorkshire, your future welfare in life depends upon yourselves! If your village has a Mechanics' Institution, join it!" More soberly he recommended a well-stocked library and a reading room supplied with newspapers, argued that classes should be formed on the principle of mutual improvement and that lectures are not without great benefit. More encouragingly for village members, he suggested a weekly practice of vocal music 'to sweeten the toils of labour with the glorious strains of Handel' and proposed that an Annual Soirée might be held 'when all may unite in innocent festivity'.

1990's - Mechanics' Institution - before house conversion

The 'Ripon and Richmond Chronicle' reported extensively on the opening ceremony including Butterfield's rousing speech:- "'What use are these Mechanics' Institutions? What good do they do in a parish? Now, I want this Institution, bursting as it is into new life coming out of the chrysalis, if I may so speak, into the higher state of existence — I want you, my friends, the members of this society, to be in yourselves an answer to this question. I want to be able to exemplify that you are an instance where Mechanics' Institutes do good (Applause). I want you, along with other well-educated societies, to do battle against the unbelievers, and show, by your conduct, a bright example of how the one great secret of doing things is, to make a proper use of the advantages here offered you: to remember that knowledge is only beneficial when it is properly applied."

"As to the music: a most excellent programme, not only promised, but afforded a rich treat. Miss Wheater, of Bradford, and Miss Carrodus, of Keighley, backed up with Sugden, Clapham, and Robinson, of the Bradford Choral Union, formed the company — having Mr. Midgley at the piano-forte. In fact, all present on the occasion will long remember the occasion of the opening of the new Mechanics' Hall in the village of Bishop Monkton, in the Parish of Ripon, in the Wapentake of Claro, in the West Riding of the Great County of York."

In the early decades of the Institution, there were many concerts and other big events which attracted people from many neighbouring places. The 'Leeds Mercury' reported in April 1864 that, remarkably, 300 people had attended the Annual Soiree. "The secluded and pleasantly situated village of Bishop Monkton was again the scene of much excitement and general interest on Monday last, on the occasion of the Annual Soirée held in the Institute hall. An excellent tea was provided, of which nearly 300 partook. The tables were presided over by the ladies of the village, who acquitted themselves with great credit - as ladies only can do. The assembly consisted of the principal inhabitants of Bishop

Monkton and many respectable parties from the neighbouring villages, and Knaresborough and Ripon."

In 1868 there was a concert by 'The Wandering Minstrels" assisted by Mr. Carrodus of Her Majesty's Opera, London. The ladies of the village once again produced tea and cakes which encouraged a high standard of baking! It was found that there was not enough room for these events and so a gallery was erected. The clock was added later with money raised by Mr. J. E. Simpson and it would go on chiming regularly for more than a century, even after the Mechanics' closed.

The 'Mickey', as it affectionately became known, continued to provide a mix of learning and culture with a Reading Room, which stocked among other things newspapers, a Library, and regular lectures and classes were held there. The great success of its first quarter of a century was proof of a thirst for learning and self-improvement. Over the years, however, and into the twentieth-century, its emphasis gradually became more about entertainment and less about education and in many ways it was the forerunner of the Village Hall. At the beginning of the twentieth-century the Mechanics' was used for flower shows, concerts, dances and whist drives and a billiard table was added, although night classes still took place. Until 1920 the Mechanics' was used by both sexes. However, the village Women's Institute was founded and thereafter, the 'Mickey' became men-only.

The building acquired other uses. It was used for the certifying of weights and measures by farmers and local shopkeepers. During the First World War, it was much frequented by soldiers. During the Second World War, the Mechanics' was used to house machinery for the fire brigade. After the War the young men of the village would gather to play billiards and have leisure time together. But, with the coming of television in the 1950s, fewer people frequented the Mechanics' and it was no longer a learning centre. Adult education was by then widely available elsewhere.

2017 - Mechanics' Institution - after house conversion

The 1970s onwards were a period of slow decline. Various attempts were made to turn the building effectively into a community centre. A pre and after school club was run there for a while. In the 1980s a youth club operated for about four years but it was difficult to find people to organise it. Many Mechanics' became libraries and museums but Bishop Monkton did not have a large enough community to warrant such a change of use.

Eventually, the Mechanics' building became part of the deal which led to the construction of the Village Hall on Knaresborough Road. After a protracted search for legal documents and a search to find who were the Trustees, it was agreed at a meeting on 7th December, 1999, to wind up the affairs of the Mechanics' Institution and to authorise the sale of the building. The proceeds of the sale, along with those of the nearby former W.I. Hall on Main Street, helped fund the new Village Hall which opened in 2005.

Sadly, the Bishop Monkton Mechanics' Institution had become a relic of a bygone age and we will never see its like again, certainly not in the form it once existed. Thereafter, the Mechanics' was turned into a house and used for holiday lets right up to the 2020s. It is now privately owned with its clockface restored and still bearing its original inscription above the front door.

AFTERWORD

Bishop Monkton School is very much alive and looking to the future.

At the time of the Millennium, in April 2000, children from the School buried a time capsule near the beck in the village. Again in 2022, as part of the Platinum Jubilee Celebrations for the late Queen Elizabeth II, they buried another time capsule, this time on the Playing Fields near the Village Hall.

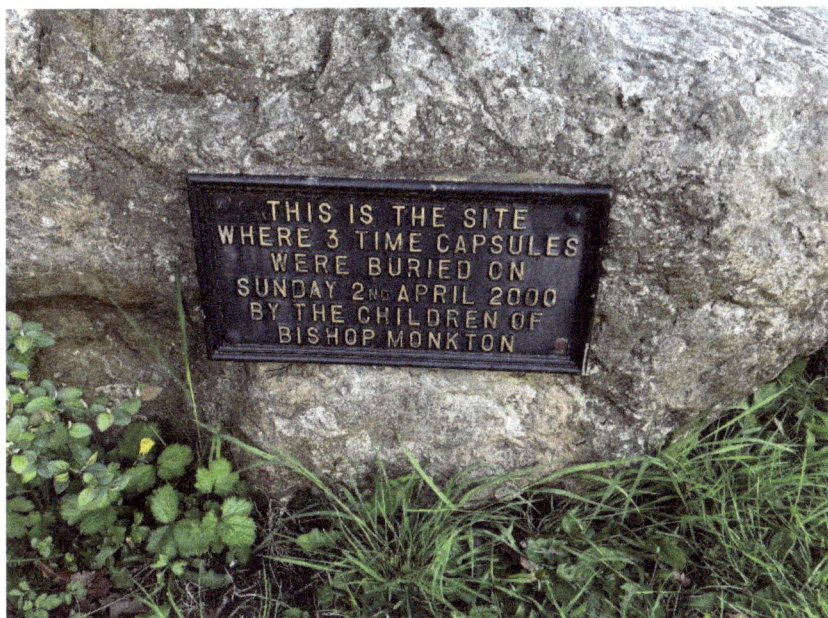

Time capsule buried by schoolchildren in 2000 to mark the Millennium

Both capsules were buried with the intention that they should be opened a hundred years after their burial. Each contained objects from everyday life. The 2022 capsule included, among other things, a copy of the Ripon Gazette from Thursday 2nd June 2022', a Covid Test (Negative), a Covid Mask (clean), a BeckBusters medal, school class photos, a chewed school pencil and a 50p coin! This demonstrates two things about the School. Firstly, that it has a strong sense of its own history. During the Autumn Term of 2024, the history of the School was a learning topic for pupils in all year groups. This included a school assembly where former pupils and staff came into School and shared their memories. Children enjoyed this tremendously and they clearly understand that they are part of a tradition which goes back almost 200 years.

2022 Jubilee - Tree planting and a Time Capsule

However, it also shows that the School is looking to the future. None of us knows exactly how Bishop Monkton will develop in the years to come. Nor do we know how educational philosophies and strategies will change. It is likely that the village will grow in size. At the time of writing, one new housing development, already with planning approval, is likely to start soon and another scheme is currently still locked in the planning process.

Whatever the outcome of this, it will almost certainly mean more young families and more children living in the village. This will provide both an opportunity and a challenge for the School. However, the evidence gathered in this book about the history of Bishop Monkton School provides confidence that what Sally Cowling describes as 'a small village school with a big heart' will continue to serve its community with distinction into the future.

2024 - Reminiscence Session

In November, the entire school was fascinated by a reminiscing session with three former pupils (Margaret Simpson (1943-46), Clare Royds (1954-57) and Susan Brown (1960's) plus teacher Mandy Coupland, who are shown here with Head Sally Cowling.

CLASS PICTURES 2025

Wrens

Robins

Owls

Kestrels

Kites

Year 6

ACKNOWLEDGEMENTS

Credits

The following people were involved in researching, writing and editing this book – Annabel Alton, Chris Bagnall, Sally Cowling, David Darbyshire, Feather Gordon, Martin Minett and Colin Philpott.

The following members of the Bishop Monkton Local History Group also contributed to the book's production – Mandy Hazel, Lizzie Darbyshire, and Hilary Philpott.

Original photography was by Hannah Knight, Rachel Bottomley and Colin Philpott. With thanks to Tempest Photography for images of classes of 2025 - www.tempest-photography.co.uk.

All members of staff and pupils at Bishop Monkton School helped with the project in a variety of ways.

The following other people generously gave their time to share their memories and expertise – Paul Jennings, the late Ada Wilkinson, David Simpson, Margaret Simpson, Elizabeth Wilkinson, Alan Chisem, Howard Morland, Clare Royds, Sue Brown, the late Doreen Willis, Sue Roome, Florence Bowes, Sarah Worthington, Christine Feeny, Carole Minett, Jen Barker, Christine Duffield, Stancey Coughlan, Oliver Coughlan, Paul Collinson, Sara Collinson.

Copyright

All archive pictures in this book are used with the permission of copyright holders where it has been possible to contact them. We have made our best efforts to do so with the information available.

Pictures showing current pupils of the school are included with the permission of their parents or guardians. Pictures of former pupils are included on the basis that anyone shown in these pictures will no longer be aged under eighteen.

Sources

North Yorkshire Archives
West Yorkshire Archives
British Library
University of Leeds Archives
National Archives, Tithe Apportionments, 1837
Bishop Monkton School, Head Teachers' Journal, 1869-1900
Bishop Monkton School, Head Teachers' Journal, 1901-1914
Bishop Monkton School, Managers' Minute Book, 1905-1956
Bishop Monkton School, Head Teachers' Journal, 1970-2009
Ancestry, www.ancestry.co.uk
The British Newspaper Archive, www.britishnewspaperarchive.co.uk
Kelly's, Post Office, and Harrod & Co. Directory, annual editions 1822-1937.
'The Times'
Gillard, Derek, *Education in the UK: a history* (2018), www.education-uk.org/history.

Newman, Mark, *The Wonder of the North: Fountains Abbey and Studley Royal* (Boydell Press for the National Trust, 2015).

Mary Gertrude Butterfield, *Bishop Monkton and its Environs*, 1958

Eddie Bowes, Monkton Matters Booklet, 1988.

Support

We are grateful to the Johnson & Mukherjee Charitable Trust and to the Two Ridings Community Foundation for their generous financial support of this project.

Other Links

Bishop Monkton Local History Group website https://bmlhg.chessck.co.uk

Bishop Monkton C of E Primary School website https://www.bishopmonkton.n-yorks.sch.uk

www.ingramcontent.com/pod-product-compliance
Lightning Source LLC
Chambersburg PA
CBHW040833110426
42739CB00037B/3489